T0299377

Smashing Glass Ceilings

Smashing Glass Ceilings is the book to help elevate and excite women across the education sector to become confident, successful and fulfilled in their careers. Empowerment can look and feel different for everyone, and this book is designed to show every woman how she can succeed in the education sector.

In addition to providing a wealth of advice about leadership progression, bestselling author and presenter Kate Jones shares guidance on alternative options to leadership for women in education. Have you ever thought about launching and hosting your own podcast about teaching and learning? Are you keen to lead professional development training internally and/or externally? Are you a keen writer but not sure how to set up a website to blog or how to get published? Helpful tips and suggestions for these routes and more are presented alongside a wide range of diverse case studies and interviews that shine a spotlight on innovative women, from school leaders to entrepreneurs in education. The book also contains advice for male colleagues so that they too can help empower women in education.

This book will provide advice, guidance and inspiration for all women in education regardless of age, role or experience.

Kate Jones is a teacher, leader, bestselling author, blogger and award-winning international speaker.

Smashing Glass Ceilings

Empowering Women in Education

Kate Jones

Routledge
Taylor & Francis Group

LONDON AND NEW YORK

Designed cover image: © Lisa Dynan

First published 2024
by Routledge
4 Park Square, Milton Park, Abingdon, Oxon OX14 4RN

and by Routledge
605 Third Avenue, New York, NY 10158

Routledge is an imprint of the Taylor & Francis Group, an informa business

British Library Cataloguing-in-Publication Data
A catalogue record for this book is available from the British Library

Library of Congress Cataloging-in-Publication Data
Names: Jones, Kate, 1987– author.
Title: Smashing glass ceilings : empowering women in education / Kate Jones.
Description: Abingdon, Oxon ; New York, NY : Routledge, 2024. |
    Includes bibliographical references and index. Identifiers:
    LCCN 2023020790 (print) | LCCN 2023020791 (ebook) |
    ISBN 9781032461977 (hardback) | ISBN 9781032461960 (paperback) |
    ISBN 9781003380528 (ebook)
Subjects: LCSH: Education—Vocational guidance—Great Britain. | Women in
    education—Great Britain. | Women—Vocational guidance—Great Britain.
Classification: LCC LB1775.4.G7 J65 2024 (print) | LCC LB1775.4.G7 (ebook) |
    DDC 370.82—dc23/eng/20230808
LC record available at https://lccn.loc.gov/2023020790
LC ebook record available at https://lccn.loc.gov/2023020791

ISBN: 978-1-032-46197-7 (hbk)
ISBN: 978-1-032-46196-0 (pbk)
ISBN: 978-1-003-38052-8 (ebk)

DOI: 10.4324/9781003380528

Typeset in Melior
by Apex CoVantage, LLC

Dedicated to a wonderful woman,
Hazel Pearson
(my Gran).

Contents

About the Author

Kate Jones is Senior Associate for Teaching and Learning with Evidence Based Education. An experienced teacher and leader, Kate has spent over a decade in the classroom, teaching in the UK and internationally in the United Arab Emirates. In addition to this, Kate has authored eight books and is the editor of the researchED Guide to Cognitive Science. She is a regular contributor to various educational magazines including *TES* (*Times Educational Supplement*). Kate is also an experienced international speaker and has presented across the UK, Middle East, Hong Kong, Singapore, Thailand, New Zealand and more. You can follow and connect with her on Instagram and Twitter @KateJones_Teach.

Acknowledgements

It is appropriate to begin thanking the women who have supported and inspired me. There are too many to mention but I do want to thank colleagues who became lifelong friends and confidants. Thank you to Jade Williams, Louise Rycroft, Danielle Malson, Sarah Findlater, Mel Davis, Jo Wallace, Rima Schooley, Becky Howarth, Morgan Whitfield Carney, Laura Brammer, and Paulette and Millie Leppard. A sincere thanks goes to my incredible best friend Hannah Bellis. Thank you to my male friends and colleagues: Tom Rogers, Dan Morrow, Nigel Davis, Mark Leppard, James McBlane, Jamie Scott and the team at Evidence Based Education.

A big thank you to the individuals who have contributed to this book. I am very grateful as their contributions have helped to shape this book and provide unique insight and wisdom. I am thrilled to include a foreword by Vivienne Porritt OBE, as she is a fantastic role model and inspiration to myself and many others in education.

As always thanks to my family. Thank you Mum and Dad, Heather and Andre and my sisters, nieces and nephew. I am very fortunate to live with such a supportive, loving and kind family. My step children Charlie and William bring so much joy, laughter and love to my life. Thank you.

Finally, the most important thank you goes to my wonderful partner Geoff. You have supported me, encouraged me and empowered me. I am so excited for the next chapter in my life with you beside me.

Foreword

Vivienne Porritt OBE

Empowering women in education is a passion of mine, and Kate Jones has done a super job in exploring this topic in a multi-faceted way. Whether you are a teacher or a leader in schools, colleges or universities or supporting educators in other ways, Kate's advice will enable you to be clear about your ambition and how to realise it.

First and foremost, I love that there are now so many women writing about education and, I hope, that the writers of bestselling education books will all be women to reflect their numbers in the workforce. Kate rightly describes the disproportionate number of women in leadership roles especially in schools, to which I would also add universities. When we started WomenEd in 2015, we did so because we wanted to give women educators and leaders a voice in discourse on social media rather than being silenced or ignored. We now have a global mission to support women to lead education. This book adds to our calls for equity for women and gives women tools to think about how they can best contribute, which may be, for example, as a teacher, a leader, a writer or a speaker.

Kate's personal story is valuable reading as are the useful profiles with women in schools and those now working in support of education. Women's stories and journeys are at the heart of WomenEd and you will recognise something of yourself in this book. Other grassroot organisations are also referenced which recognises the diversity of women for whom the ceiling *'is not made of glass but of concrete'*.[1] There are also reminders that women can still struggle with acknowledging their own accomplishments or with imposter syndrome and so we dim or lose our voice. This book will support you to find your voice and put it to good use in the right role for you.

In the final chapter, Patrick Ottley-O'Connor highlights the importance of deeds and actions to match our words, and Kate Jones has given a multitude of ways in which you can be empowered. This is the most important message of the book, to me. Women need to reject the ceilings they may face and decide how they want to be empowered as individuals. This does not mean we need to fix women, rather we are calling out the stereotypes and the gendered perceptions that frame how women are seen whilst also tackling systemic inequities. However, if we wait for these inequities to be fully addressed, our daughters and their daughters may face the same challenges. We can accelerate the pace and bring about much needed change by ourselves and by connecting and collaborating with other women. We can be 10% braver by becoming empowered and choosing our own way forward.

Vivienne Porritt OBE
Co-founder and Global Strategic Leader of WomenEd

Endnote

1 Porritt, V., & Featherstone, K. (2019). *10% braver: Inspiring women to lead education.* Page 58.

Introduction

This book aims to do exactly what it states on the cover: **empower women in education.** Empowering women in education isn't just about promoting women into leadership positions, although that is an important and significant element of this book. Being empowered can look and feel very different for every woman.

Empowerment can involve leadership at different levels but it can also involve more women writing, speaking and presenting about education and issues or topics they feel strongly about. Being empowered could involve successfully balancing family life with a rewarding and fulfilling career in the classroom. Ambition can come in many forms; from promotion, earning more money, gaining a profile within the education community, becoming an established author or something else.

Teaching has historically been viewed as a female dominated profession and not just in the UK. Referring to female teachers in the US Womenscolleges.org/history states:

> Colleges began enrolling women students in the mid 19th century. The earliest undergraduates anticipated using their degrees to become better wives and mothers. However, a critical need for school teachers arose as public education expanded throughout the country. Women (based on the popular belief that they were more nurturing than men) were seen as the ideal candidates to fill the need. Colleges expanded their teacher training programs and encouraged their female students to enrol at the expense of other majors.

The article continues:

> In 2014, women earned 80% of the Bachelor's degrees in Education, creating a female-dominated candidate pool for new teaching positions. Women began earning advanced degrees more than 150 years ago, and they were encouraged to use their expanded knowledge as teachers. The legacy of teaching as a woman's profession remains deeply embedded in US culture.[1]

DOI: 10.4324/9781003380528-1

The School Workforce census collects data and information from schools and local authorities on the school workforce in state-funded schools in England. Independent schools, non-maintained special schools, sixth-form colleges and further education establishments are not included in the report. The report published in June 2022 by the School Workforce in England stated, *'School workforce ethnic diversity is increasing, but the teaching workforce continues to be predominantly female'.*[2]

When analysing teacher characteristics it was reported:

> The teaching workforce of England is consistently predominantly female; 75.5% as at November 2021 (2021/22), up from 74.4% in 2010/11. Male teachers are more likely to work in secondary schools than nurseries and primary schools: 14.1% of nursery and primary school teachers are male, up from 12.7% in 2010/11. 35.3% of secondary school teachers are male, down from 37.8% in 2010/11.

The report also commented on leadership positions in the school workforce adding: *'Female teachers are less likely than their male counterparts to be in leadership positions (heads, deputy heads, assistant heads), however this difference is reducing over time. In 2021/22, 69.4% of leadership teachers were female, up from 65.9% in 2010/11'.*

According to the Schools in Scotland statistics, published in December 2022, there are significantly more female teachers than male, especially in the primary sector where 89% of teachers are female.[3] The published data shows:

> whilst there are more female teachers than male across most sectors and grades, the difference was less pronounced in promoted posts (Deputy Head teacher or Head teachers). An exception to this is secondary schools where 65% of teachers at all grades were female compared to 43% of head teachers.[4]

In Wales, the Education Workforce Council published their statistics and key findings for 2022. The statistics originate from the Register of Education Practitioners. It is noted in Wales that, *'The majority of school teachers are female (75.5%). The gender balance is stable with little change year on year'.* However with Further Education (FE) *'the gender split is different to the other registrant groups with a higher proportion of males: 59.6% female; 40.4% male'.*[5] Despite the difference, once again the data illustrate the dominance of women across the sector.

The education workforce statistics illustrate for 2021–2022 in Northern Ireland teaching is a female dominated profession. The report notes:

> The teacher headcount is 20,936, this represents an increase of 526 teachers from 2020/21. The headcount of male teachers in 2021/22 is 4,779, this is an increase of 122 from last year. The proportion of teachers working in all schools who are male has been declining between 2017/18 and 2021/22.[6]

Other interesting statistics show a breakdown of data in Northern Ireland and the proportions of teachers that are female are 100% at Nursery, 84% at Preparatory and Primary, 71.4% at Non-Grammar, 67.7% at Grammar and 80.2% at Special School[7]. The statistics for all home counties are available publicly online to access and view. They are published online annually.

The gender pay gap (GPG), an equality measure to highlight the difference in terms of payment between men and women, remains a problem. The official government website states, *'The UK gender pay gap is at its lowest level ever – just over 18%. The gender pay gap does not show differences in pay for comparable jobs. Unequal pay for men and women has been illegal for 45 years'.*[8] The reasons for this GPG are complex and varied.

The government website explains different reasons for the GPG:

A higher proportion of women choose occupations that offer less financial reward for example, in administration. Many high-paying sectors are disproportionately made up of male workers, for example, information and communications technology. A much higher proportion of women work part-time, and part-time workers earn less than their full-time counterparts on average. Women are still less likely to progress up the career ladder into high-paying senior roles.[9]

The observations are not specifically referring to the education sector, or any single profession, but rather the GPG nationally. However, the points raised can be applied to women in education.

The British government are taking actions to recognise and address the GPG but further transparency and openness about pay and salary across the profession will help significantly. The government website states they are taking action through the following:

- *Requiring large employers, including the public sector, to publish their gender pay gap and gender bonus gap.*

- *Offering 30 hours of free childcare for working families with 3- and 4-year-olds.*

- *Encouraging girls to consider a wider range of careers, including in those higher paying sectors traditionally dominated by men.*

The GOV.UK website states that the government has already:

- *Extended the right to request flexible working to all employees.*

- *Introduced shared parental leave.*

- *Commissioned a review to look at how we can remove the barriers preventing women getting to the top of their careers.*

The GPG should not be an issue in 2023 yet it remains so. If branching out to leading professional development or authoring a book, how do we ensure that women are paid a fair amount and guarantee it is equal to their male counterparts? This is not only a problem that needs to be addressed whilst women are at work, as the GPG naturally extends to pensions too. On International Women's Day 2023, March 8th, Scottish Widows tweeted @ScottishWidows, *'Our research shows that on average, women today retire with £123k less than men. The gap has widened with persistent imbalances in pay, caring responsibilities and part-time work impacting women's retirement savings'*.

There are lots of financial decisions for women to consider such as maternity pay, childcare, pensions and more. No book can contain all the answers but I have aimed to increase awareness, knowledge and understanding of these important issues.

Despite the historical and contemporary data only in recent years has the significance and importance of women in education been discussed publicly and widely. The phenomenal WomenEd movement has been a powerful driving force for good and continues to be. WomenEd is a global grassroots movement to connect aspiring and existing female leaders in education and provide female leaders in education a voice that can be heard. The movement continues to gain traction and interest around the world, but despite their huge success there is still more work to do to empower women in education.

I am one of many women inspired by the WomenEd movement. I began my teaching career, training and then qualifying as a secondary teacher of history in 2010 in Wales at the age of 21. I found teaching an extremely difficult and demanding job. I struggled to maintain any glimpse of work-life balance. I worried about whether I could be a teacher long term because I didn't believe it was a sustainable career. I recall the admiration I felt for colleagues with partners and children because I couldn't fathom how I would manage a relationship (let alone children) with the demands of the job.

The school where I taught as a Newly Qualified Teacher (NQT) was the school where I remained for the initial five years of my career. During that time I became Head of Department and I took on various whole school leadership responsibilities and roles. This school did encourage and enable me to flourish professionally. It was an environment where it was possible to share my passion, knowledge and expertise with colleagues and further afield. This was due to the supportive and enthusiastic Senior Leadership Team (SLT).

In 2016, I relocated to Abu Dhabi in the United Arab Emirates to teach in a British curriculum school. This was a nerve wracking yet exciting adventure, linked to my love of travel and exploring. During the five years I spent as a single woman living and working in the Middle East region, I met wonderful people, from students to colleagues and people I consider to be lifelong friends.

During this period I was very fortunate to travel the world visiting exotic locations including the Philippines, India, Maldives and more. I also gained financially as the salary for teachers in the Middle East is considerably higher than in the UK. The wage is tax free with the majority of schools providing employees with rent-free accommodation, private medical insurance, annual flights and other generous benefits.

There were many challenges I encountered during this time abroad, both professional and personal. It can be difficult to separate the two when the struggles negatively impact mental health. In the first two years teaching and living abroad I experienced a lot of setbacks, and despite many attempts at applying for a promotion, each time I was unsuccessful. I was very ambitious and hardworking but realised a promotion was not going to happen at my school. It was then I decided to take control of my career, success and wellbeing. I recognised a change was needed.

In 2018 my first book, *Love to Teach: Research and Resources for Every Classroom* (John Catt Publishing Ltd) was published. The publishing contract was a result of sharing teaching and learning ideas for the classroom on social media. I also gained experience writing blogs and articles for various educational publications. This was an excellent starting point in terms of writing about education. I gained an audience and my ideas, resources and advice were proving to be useful and helpful for other teachers.

Following the publication of my book I was invited to speak at prestigious events across the Middle East and other countries such as Hong Kong, as well as events in the UK. I was an author and public speaker in addition to my full-time teaching role. In 2019 I gained a promotion from classroom teacher to Head of History at a different British curriculum school in Abu Dhabi. I continued to write, present and branch out.

I authored a series of books focusing on Retrieval Practice in the classroom.[10] I have been successful as an Amazon best-selling author. Writing is a passion that has taken me by surprise, as I never planned or intended to write but I feel incredibly lucky I can combine my two loves; education and writing.

This is my eighth book, and I am currently editing a book with further publications planned for the future. There has been a boom in recent years with classroom practitioners and school leaders authoring books. This is brilliant as it is vital to hear and learn from those working on the ground. Despite this influx of voices at the chalkface, the Amazon education charts show the field is still dominated by male authors. There is a rise in female authors but there needs to be more representation and more female voices in education being published.

In addition to writing about education, I continue to speak at educational events in the UK, internationally and online. I have launched my own podcast, hosted my own radio show aimed at teachers and had the privilege to collaborate with leading voices in the field of education. I am now Senior Associate for Teaching and Learning with Evidence Based Education, working three days a week and using the rest of my time to focus on other projects including consultancy.

I regularly work with schools, leading inset training and twilight sessions for professional development and I enjoy this immensely. I am very active on social media with a following of over 55,000 on Twitter (at the time of writing). I am gradually building up my profile across other platforms such as LinkedIn, Instagram, Facebook and YouTube. Throughout this book I aim to combine evidence from research with my own experiences and the experiences of others involved in education.

A critique was raised over my ability to write this book about empowering women as I am not an experienced senior leader and have not led a school as Headteacher or CEO. This narrow view suggests success is defined as leadership, a belief I regularly challenge. Despite not leading a school or Multi Academy Trust, I am very proud of my thriving and accomplished career.

Leadership is certainly a route to promotion, more money and status but it is not the only way women can be successful and empowered in education. There are now many alternatives and this book will explore those. There are books, blogs and presentations encouraging women to be 10% braver (a mantra created and promoted by the WomenEd movement to motivate and inspire women in education). This book offers practical and concrete advice as to how women can be braver in the process of becoming empowered.

Throughout my career as I gained experience I also grew in confidence but this was over a significant period of time. Maintaining balance between a happy professional and personal life can at times still be tough. At the time of writing I am in a very loving relationship and expecting my first child, I am delighted we are having a daughter. This has provided me with a new perspective because I hope my daughter does not face obstacles and barriers but can thrive in a society where women are celebrated and empowered.

I have considered the possibility of becoming a mother for a long time but wondered and worried about the impact it could have on my career. I am not alone with these fears as research has been published about the 'motherhood penalty', (discussed further in Chapter 8) referring to the negative impact parenthood can have on women and their career.

Women should not have to make a choice or sacrifice. It is very possible, although it is not always easy, to have a fulfilling professional and personal life. An empowered woman is a happy woman, in control of her life and content with the decisions and choices she has made.

Securing the right role, whether in a school or outside of a school working in education, is crucial to wellbeing and fulfilment, therefore it is vital to get that right. Leadership can be incredibly rewarding and as the WomenEd movement has shown, there should be more female leaders in education and their voices should be given a platform to be heard. Leading and delivering professional development can be gratifying and financially lucrative. There are women in education who have demonstrated innovation and ambition, taking risks and reaping the rewards. If there are to be more female writers in education, how do we make that happen? The process of writing for a magazine, setting up a blog or becoming a published author is explored in this book along with the factors mentioned above.

Public speaking is a key skill in education; whether that involves speaking in front of a class of students, addressing colleagues in a staff meeting or delivering a whole school assembly. There are also opportunities for women to speak at educational events but again this is not always easy or straightforward. Advice, guidance and tips related to public speaking feature as a chapter in this book. In order for more women in education to be heard, women have to have the opportunity to speak. Women need to be invited to and celebrated at educational events. Women then need to seize those opportunities.

There are other issues explored in this book that are important but not as widely discussed; for example how does someone gain a profile and following on social media? Why is that important? How do authors self-promote their work? How should leaders celebrate their achievements and the success of others? Social media offers other platforms for women to be heard in education and having a social media presence can bring with it many benefits (as well as challenges).

Throughout the book are a series of interviews and case studies written by women and men in education who have kindly agreed to share their thoughts, guidance and reflections. There are also examples of women in the 'spotlight', as I am keen to shine a light on empowered women in education and share their success stories. Where there are gaps in my experience or knowledge, I have invited those who possess expertise in those areas to share their wisdom, experiences and advice. I am very grateful to all those who have contributed to this book.

This book is written for all women in education. Regardless of age, background, position, title or experience. This book aims to be inclusive and contains a wide range of diverse voices. There needs to be support for women new to the profession trying to navigate and adapt as I did. Experienced female teachers and leaders need to be given a platform to share. There also needs to be inclusion of women of colour, trans women, LGBTQ+, pregnant women and mothers, carers, women that experience learning difficulties or physical disabilities, victims of abuse, women experiencing menopause and those reaching their end of career.

This book isn't written just for women. There needs to be a male audience because as the final chapter shows, it is essential everyone supports and helps to empower women in education.

Throughout my career I have experienced professional jealousy from colleagues. I have been mocked for being invested in my career with accusations of 'not having a life' or being a 'workaholic'. I have been given unhelpful and unsolicited advice as have many other women.

I have also been very fortunate to have worked with colleagues and leaders who have acted as mentors and sources of support or inspiration (male and female). We can encourage or discourage others. We don't have a choice over how people treat us but we do have a choice on how we treat others. We should always aim to empower those around us whether they be our students or colleagues.

Kate

#SmashingGlassCeilings

Endnotes

1 https://www.womenshistory.org/articles/why-are-so-many-teachers-women.
2 https://explore-education-statistics.service.gov.uk/find-statistics/school-workforce-in-england.
3 https://www.gov.scot/publications/summary-statistics-for-schools-in-scotland-2022/pages/school-teachers/.
4 https://www.statista.com/statistics/718481/number-of-schools-in-scotland/#:~:text= Published%20by%20D.%20Clark%2C%20Jan%20%2024%2C%202023%20There,in%20 Scotland%20and%20a%20further%20109%20special%20schools.
5 https://www.ewc.wales/site/index.php/en/research-and-statistics/workforce-statistics.html.
6 https://www.education-ni.gov.uk/publications/teacher-workforce-statistics-202122.
7 https://www.education-ni.gov.uk/sites/default/files/publications/education/Teacher%20 workforce%20statistical%20infographic%20202122.PDF.
8 https://www.gov.uk/government/news/uk-gender-pay-gap.
9 https://www.gov.uk/government/news/uk-gender-pay-gap.
10 Retrieval practice is the act of recalling information from long term-memory to strengthen memory and therefore support learning.

# Securing the right role

Securing the right role in education, inside or outside of a school environment, has to be the starting point of this book. It is central to ensuring a happy, fulfilled and rewarding professional life. This can involve securing the right role at the start of a teaching career or it can be when a woman has reached a point when she is ready for a professional or personal change or to take the next steps with career development.

There are many factors to consider when planning and applying for the right role. There can also be challenges and obstacles to overcome. The tide is turning with more discussion of promoting, supporting and empowering women into leadership but there is still much to be done. This is explored with a specific focus on women in leadership in the next chapter.

I have worked in three schools (excluding the schools in which I have trained, for a brief period during my Initial Teacher Training). I am very fortunate to have worked at two wonderful schools (not perfect, but no school is). During that time I worked with people who supported me and encouraged me to achieve my potential. These were schools that enhanced my professional development and enabled me to grow in confidence as a teacher.

I have also spent time at a school where I was very unhappy. I did not agree with the ethics and ethos the school promoted. There was a culture of nepotism and sexism that I struggled to challenge, despite my efforts. Staff retention and staff morale was extremely low. There were daily challenges, different to the challenges I experienced in my previous places of work. These challenges took a toll on my health and wellbeing. This school made me consider leaving education to find an alternative career, but I made the decision to leave the school, not the profession.

Leaving behind the struggles at this school gave me a newfound appreciation for my next school and the colleagues I worked with. I reflect on this time in my career as a low point, both professionally and personally. My experience may not be common but it is not unique. The importance of securing the right role should not be underestimated but instead given very thoughtful care and consideration.

DOI: 10.4324/9781003380528-2

Recent figures published by the National Foundation for Educational Research (NFER) show in England the government has missed the target for recruitment of secondary school teachers in 2022, 41% below target and for the first time, the recruitment of trainee primary teachers is 7% below target.[1] The recruitment and retention crisis the profession is currently experiencing across the UK suggests teaching is not as alluring as it once was and many are choosing to leave the profession for various reasons. If more teachers felt happier and content in their roles and at their school, would that make a difference? Possibly, although there are also national contributors such as funding, pay and workload which play a part too.

It's not always easy leaving a job, even if you are unhappy and unfulfilled. Financial commitments and the risk of the grass not always being greener can be factors at play. An experienced classroom teacher is an asset to the profession. They possess knowledge, insight and understanding that only someone who has spent significant time in the classroom can secure. However, as teachers rise through the pay scale with classroom experience they become more expensive and the reality is, schools are struggling with their budgets. Experienced teachers should be treasured, not disregarded because they are more costly to hire.

There are issues unique to women, for example, moving schools or taking on a new role can impact maternity pay and support. The application process can be daunting, taxing and prevent people from leaving their current position and school. Despite challenges and obstacles, it is possible to secure the right role.

Case study: Securing the right role

Below is an inspirational case study from a school leader, who has requested to remain anonymous. The experience shared below shows how a female leader in education was able to take control of her career progression and not compromise when applying for the right role. She was able to secure the right role, a dream role, despite many challenges and worries she faced.

After years of battling infertility, I took the decision to try IVF in January 2022. This was a tough decision to make because I was aware from speaking to other women who had received fertility treatment that it can be emotionally and physically draining. It took years for me to pursue treatment because I couldn't see how I would juggle it with work. My career is important to me; it got me through the dark days of infertility. However, there was so much unpredictability about IVF treatment. Hospital appointments couldn't be neatly calendared, and time off couldn't be organised in advance. I would have to inject at set times each day, and medication had to be kept refrigerated.

My role as a MAT (Multi Academy Trust) Executive Leader required me to travel across the country and I couldn't see how I would continue in my role as I had been and go through fertility treatment. It wasn't until I spoke to a friend who had been through this, I realised it was impossible to go through IVF and work in the way

I had been and that was okay. In fact, it was necessary to make changes to maximise my chance of success. The truth is, if I hadn't accepted this, I would have never felt ready.

My doctor mapped out the course of treatment. We discussed the periods when I would need to take time off work and he wrote a letter communicating to this effect for my employer. This was very helpful, and I met with my line manager to discuss it. He was extremely compassionate. We agreed I would work from home during my treatment. The Covid-19 pandemic had given us a blueprint for how this could work. We also discussed how I would communicate this change to my colleagues. This was an important conversation to have. We agreed I would tell them I had to have a small operation and I needed to be isolated.

I made my team aware that I was going through IVF, and informed them they might need to step into meetings or deliver training on my behalf with short notice. Airing this unpredictability felt like a massive weight had been lifted. Moreover, being vulnerable opened up conversations about how we might support other colleagues experiencing infertility. It led to a review of the leave of absence policy and conversations with principals about how we can better support each other.

Sadly, not everyone experiences this level of support. Since sharing my story, women have reached out and told me they had to fight for time off and 'make up the hours' when attending appointments because fertility appointments are not an entitlement in the leave of absence policy. Undertaking fertility treatment is stressful enough without having to plead for the time off!

I qualified as a teacher 16 years ago and, since then, have been fortunate enough to have many wonderful opportunities. Whilst exploring fertility treatment, I had also started to think about what might be next for me in my career. The years of infertility had left me feeling in limbo, and every new role felt risky in case all my dreams came true and I became pregnant. In March 2022 all my dreams did come true because I found out the IVF had worked. I decided to put my career on the back burner because the idea of taking on a new role and becoming a mother seemed incompatible.

In June 2022 I saw my dream role advertised: an Executive Director at a prestigious Institute of Teaching. I felt excited and gutted at the same time. I wanted both: to be a mother and to have my dream job, which should be entirely attainable for every woman. But it felt impossible.

I talked it through with family and friends but felt like I was hitting a dead end. I was advised to focus on my pregnancy and not go through any big changes because having a baby would be enough! My baby would be my priority but I also wanted to apply for the job. I wished the role had been advertised a year later because I felt if I did apply and was successful, I'd be letting my new employer down by leaving to go on maternity leave. I couldn't imagine how it would work because I had no direct experience of seeing women move into new roles and then go on maternity in the first year. I also thought that even if I applied, I probably wouldn't be successful as soon as I declared my pregnancy. I've heard horror stories about women who have not been appointed because they were at 'childbearing age', so the fact I was pregnant felt like a massive disadvantage.

Despite all my concerns, I couldn't shake the excitement for the role and, after much hesitation, I applied. I was convinced my application wouldn't progress once they found out I was pregnant, but I felt better for applying.

Later that week I had lunch with a friend who works in HR and I discussed this with her. She was delighted for me, but I was crushed when she told me that if I changed employer whilst pregnant, I wouldn't be entitled to statutory maternity pay. The best I could hope for was a maternity allowance. I wouldn't say statutory maternity pay is generous, but the maternity allowance is almost impossible to survive on!

I started to do the maths and wondered if we could make it work but I couldn't help feeling angry as this role felt perfect for me. I didn't want to choose between being able to afford to care for my baby and the dream job. I decided I was not prepared to suffer this financial penalty, but I wasn't prepared to give up.

I wrote to the Academy Trust advertising the role and made them aware I was pregnant. I told them this did not change my enthusiasm for the role and asked about their maternity policy and any financial implications if I was successful. I had to trust there would be no maternity bias applied to my application.

On receiving my email, the CEO of the MAT reviewed the maternity guidance and discovered there was a significant financial disadvantage to colleagues who joined whilst pregnant. He was clear this did not seem fair and discussed the maternity guidance with an employment solicitor who advised him there was no legal reason why he couldn't waive the requirement for a new colleague to be employed by the MAT for a set period of time in order to receive occupational maternity benefits.

He then spoke to the Chair and Vice-Chair of the Trust Board who agreed they should change this discriminatory policy to ensure colleagues who join the Trust whilst pregnant are not penalised. I couldn't believe that one email had triggered a chain of events that led to the Trust Board agreeing, unanimously, to an immediate change of policy for all employees at the MAT! Regardless of whether I was successful in my application, this was a massive win and I wish all organisations were this inclusive.

When it came to the shortlisting process, the CEO informed me he didn't declare to the panel that I was 18 weeks pregnant; he said it was 'irrelevant'. Shortly after, I was delighted to find out that I had been shortlisted. The CEO and I agreed he would tell the selection panels on the morning of the interviews that I was pregnant (as it would be obvious when I entered the room!).

On the day of the interview, I still convinced myself that I was unlikely to be appointed as my pregnancy would be too big of a hurdle to overcome. However, to my surprise, I was appointed and started the role in September 2022 at thirty weeks pregnant.

Taking on the role meant a new and unexpected (but welcome) challenge. How would I strategically lead a new project and keep its momentum whilst on maternity leave? I began envisioning trying to look after a baby and run the project on my maternity leave. However, the CEO was adamant this would not happen, and we discussed what resources I would need so that the strategy could be implemented, and I could take precious time to care for my baby.

Being able to discuss this was important as there is no blueprint for this situation. It was important to feel there was enough psychological safety for me to talk to the CEO and say, 'This is concerning me; I don't yet know what the answer is'.

During these discussions we devised a plan whereby I would go through the usual induction of learning about the Trust and our thirty-seven academies and engaging in conversations with colleagues about the existing training and developing practices.

This allowed us to develop a clear idea from the start about what we wanted the Institute to offer and how it would be built so that we could create a dedicated development strategy with the intention of launching the Institute in September 2023, when I return from maternity leave. However, this still required someone else to come in and develop this strategy whilst I was on leave.

The outcome was a recognition that we needed to hire two more people – a Deputy Director and a Director of Programmes – to continue the work in my absence, and then continue to work alongside me when I returned. These roles were already in the development strategy but bringing them forward meant I could go on maternity leave knowing the project was in good hands and on track for when I returned.

The steps the MAT took to ensure I wouldn't be financially penalised meant I could start my new role and afford to take the time I needed to look after my little girl born in October 2022. I'm also delighted that changes to their maternity policy mean any woman who is pregnant and wishes to pursue a career at the MAT will not be financially penalised.

While the outcome achieved here has worked out well and led to a notable change in the policies, it is disappointing in a way that it would be considered 'progressive' or 'innovative'. Unfortunately, when I announced my promotion online, I was sad to receive messages from women who had been discriminated against because they were pregnant. I heard stories such as a woman who had an offer of employment retracted when she told her new employer she was pregnant, a woman who didn't apply for her dream job because she couldn't afford to take the financial hit and a woman who was struggling to survive on the maternity allowance because she changed employer. I can't help but be filled with despair that women are still having to choose between advancing their career and having children.

One day I hope this is the norm and we remove another of the many barriers that impede a mother and progress in her career. Until then we need greater visibility of these case studies to show there are ways we can improve things for women so the choice is not between a career or having children but balancing both to work for the benefit of all.

Thank you to the contributor for sharing her experiences and hopefully the attitude and approaches modelled by the MAT in the case study can lead the way and inspire change.

What is the right role for you?

When considering the right role and what that looks like to you, it is important to reflect on your current role and overall wellbeing.

Consider the following questions:

- Do you enjoy your current role? If so, what do you enjoy? If not, what do you not enjoy?
- Do you feel supported in your current role?
- Do you feel fulfilled?
- Are you professionally challenged and are you continually improving and learning?
- Is the school/working environment a place where you can flourish and develop?
- Does your role/school enable you to achieve balance with your personal and professional life?
- Are you happy with your salary?
- Are you considering or looking for a promotion?
- What is your long-term career plan and are you on track?

If you are happy in your current role and your current place of work, reflection is still very important as it can help with continued appreciation and gratitude. At this moment you may not be considering a new role, school or opportunity, but this chapter may be of value to you at a later point in your career as life events, circumstances and experiences change.

Applying for the right role

Every teacher is familiar with the application process as it begins prior to Initial Teaching Training. There is no generic application form, and different schools have differing requirements from a CV to application form to letter of application. If a school is requesting all or more than one of those forms of application, the challenge is to avoid repeating the contents of a CV on an application form or cover letter. This can be very time consuming but it is important to continually be aware that if you secure the right role then the time, effort and energy invested in the application process is worth it.

A newly qualified teacher can be desperate to secure their first teaching role and sometimes the determining factor can be location. I began my teaching career in my early twenties and during that time I lived with my parents. I could not drive therefore I was restricted to a specific area in terms of the schools in which I applied. This was not a problem because I wanted to live close to friends and family, therefore the right school for me had to be local. As this was the area in which I had lived all my life (apart from University), I had good knowledge of the area and local schools. This can be an advantage when applying for a job within a specific region but it does limit the opportunities available. If someone is willing and able to move, then this opens many more doors to explore with job opportunities.

Regardless of applying for a job as a newly qualified teacher or an experienced teacher/leader, insight about the school context is key. A school website only provides a snapshot, as can an inspection report. A school visit may not always be possible but it is highly advisable. Visiting a school during term time can be very revealing and could help inform your decision about a potential application. A visit to the school could lead to two outcomes, the school is or is not a place where you would like to work at. If the school is not right for you then time invested in the process of research, application and interview will not have been wasted.

When visiting a school, the first point to observe is the arrival process because every school has safeguarding responsibilities. Individuals should not be able to enter the school site and wander freely without signing in. A DBS (Disclosure and Barring Service) certificate is often requested if children are in the building, and this is something every school should take very seriously.

School displays, awards and notices tend to draw the attention of visitors but it's the behaviour, culture, routines and approach to professional learning that can and should be observed. First impressions count but they don't always provide the full picture. If you are able to receive a tour of the school from students or a member of staff, that can also be another great opportunity to learn through asking questions and carefully listening to responses.

Another factor to consider when applying to a new school is the way a school communicates. When contacting the school to request a school visit, or during the application process, pay attention to the communication. Any information and instructions about a visit or position advertised should be clear and concise. It is also important that information is advertised, responded to and communicated in a timely manner. For example, there should be a sufficient amount of time before the deadline for an application closes in order to give candidates time to research, prepare and complete their application.

If a candidate is successful and invited to interview, then again this should be communicated in a timely fashion to enable the candidate to make arrangements, either with lesson cover or to make travel or childcare arrangements. In terms of the interview if a presentation, assembly or lesson is required then once again time must be provided. This shows a respect and awareness of workload and respect for balance with a professional and personal life.

If a school does not give enough time to allow a candidate to prepare, then this could be a reflection of their approach to workload and deadlines at the school. This does not also take into consideration family life and other responsibilities many women have. An interview can be a nerve-wracking experience; adding further pressure and workload may suggest a warning sign not to be ignored but instead discussed, challenged or avoided.

In terms of an internal application and internal promotion, there are also factors to think about carefully. First and foremost, do you wish to stay at the current school? Is the position more attractive than the prospect of staying at your current school? Would you prefer the role at a different school? Do you believe your chances are greater at securing a promotion internally rather than externally? Accepting an internal promotion will mean the likelihood of staying at your current school for at least one academic year or possibly longer.

Another often overlooked factor about internal applications is the possibility of not securing the role. When someone is unsuccessful as an external candidate, it can be bitterly disappointing, but the upside is that they don't have to return to that school to work and they don't have to work alongside the successful candidate. Internal candidates do not have that advantage.

An unsuccessful internal candidate can feel an extra layer of hurt, disappointment or bitterness because they have been unsuccessful in their current workplace. It can be difficult to accept that we are not viewed as the best candidate. We may disagree with the decision made but it has to be accepted and respected. Colleagues are often aware of who has applied for positions and this can cause a degree of embarrassment. The unsuccessful internal candidate may have to work alongside or be line managed by the person who secured the job over them, potentially leading to resentment and tension.

Applying for any position should be considered carefully in terms of the position and school/workplace. Although it is not possible to predict outcomes, it can be useful to plan ahead and be mindful of all the potential outcomes.

Once the decision is made to apply for a position, it is crucial to ensure the application highlights your strengths, areas of expertise and experience in addition to the desire to learn and professionally develop. Fear of sounding arrogant or the lurking 'imposter syndrome' (a sense of inferiority with feelings of self-doubt, incompetence and fraud) can lead to a modest application that isn't a true reflection of your capability and potential.

An external candidate is unknown so it is important for character, personality traits and qualities to be visible in the application, alongside the relevant experience and knowledge. An internal candidate does have the advantage of knowing the school and being known in the school but that doesn't mean an application should be informal or show a lack of effort. There may be qualities, experiences and expertise you possess that are unknown, and an internal application can provide an opportunity to showcase these. Regardless whether you are an internal or external candidate the main aim of the application is to convince the employer you are the best candidate for the position.

The CV

School leaders will view a large number of CVs. They are looking for examples of individual CVs that stand out from the crowd and for positive reasons. The overall layout, presentation and design should be clear, professional and kept to at most two pages (as you progress through your career it can become challenging to include all content on two pages but ensure the two pages are kept to). The font and format should be clean and legible. The CV should also be neatly structured using bold headings and subheadings.

A common mistake is to only update a CV when applying for a new role, but it is much better to regularly update a CV with new qualifications, experiences, professional development, roles and responsibilities. This can be a useful reflection task and can be done termly or annually. It can also be useful to ask your colleagues, friends or family members to view your CV. They may remind you of something you have forgotten or they can give advice about the contents, structure and design. Another helpful strategy could be to ask others to view their CV. This could provide inspiration in terms of how they present themselves and share their expertise and experiences.

If it is a struggle to contain information to two pages, then consider saving some of the content and including that in the letter of application or application form. In terms of the content, keep the job description in mind and ensure the content is focused and relevant to the role. This will avoid repetition and can be an opportunity to include additional information or elaborate on points mentioned in your CV.

If you do not have the capacity to explore and explain points on your CV, then this can be done at interview. Keep the headlines and key points on the CV. Examples can be shared at a later date if the potential employer wants to learn more. If employers have a large number of CVs to review they may skim and scan, so ensure the content you want to be seen is made clear and bold.

It can be tempting to make a CV colourful and look stylish but this can make a CV stand out for the wrong reasons. A CV can be an opportunity to demonstrate technical skills (for example if it is a digital CV hyperlinks could be included) but the design should not distract from the content. Both style and substance are important but the substance is key.

The application form or letter of application

A CV can be generic and does not need to be tailored to the specific school and role. An application form or letter of application is different and should be original, bespoke and relevant to the position and school. A template can help with structure and content but replicating a letter of application from one school to another is a bad idea and this could be clear to the potential employer when reading the application. The application must show an understanding of the role, responsibilities and school. It should also showcase how you are suitable and ready for that position. This will draw on your skills, achievements, experience and what unique qualities and attributes you can bring to the role.

Continually refer to the job description and information you have about the school. The applicant should aim to show alignment between themselves and the role they hope to secure. Ambition is not a dirty word and this is not the time to be shy. Be bold in expressing your desire for the role. Although it is vital to air your experiences, skills and knowledge, it is not a weakness to identify areas for development and improvement. This demonstrates an ability to reflect, willingness to learn and shows self-awareness. However, don't dwell on areas of weakness as this is a job application and is a time to shine.

Do not send an application or letter without thoroughly checking and correcting it first. It is worthwhile asking someone else to view your application as they may spot errors and spelling or grammar mistakes that you didn't.

During the application process for my previous role, I was determined to get the job. I invested a lot of time in the application. I also contacted several people I knew, ranging from middle leaders to Headteachers and sought their feedback. By the time I sent my letter of application I was very proud of it. I was told at the interview my application was impressive and it was clear I had thought carefully about the role and school.

The interview process

Some schools contact candidates to inform them they have not been successful in reaching the interview stages but not all schools do so. Different schools work at different paces, therefore it could be worth following up an application to ensure it has been received and to seek confirmation about whether or not the application has been shortlisted. Securing an interview is a great next step, but again it does not secure the role, there is more work to be done!

I once experienced two job interviews in one day, at two different schools both for the positions of Head of Department. There was a stark contrast between the interviews, one a very positive experience and the other a negative encounter. The interviews helped me decide which school I wanted to work with.

The first interview was conducted by the female Headteacher and male Deputy Headteacher. They made me feel very welcome and they were both friendly and warm. I was able to relax quickly and the interview was actually very enjoyable. Prior to the questioning part of the interview I had to deliver a ten-minute presentation focusing on my vision as Head of Department, describing goals for the first year, third and fifth years. I had prepared this presentation thoroughly. I was very happy with my delivery and the interviewers listened attentively and asked me to elaborate on points they found interesting.

During the questioning part of the interview there were questions that were to be expected, for example about safeguarding, and other questions that I found challenging but to which I was able to respond. The questions focused on evidence-informed practice, professional learning, relationships with colleagues, students and parents, and they gave me a clear sense of the school's priorities. I was not told during the interview if I was successful or not, as other candidates needed to be interviewed, but I left that interview feeling very confident and happy. I genuinely felt that if I was not successful, the interview itself was a great experience.

My second interview was in the afternoon. I was interviewed by two male senior leaders including the Headteacher but I found this interview to be awful. Classical music was played in the office where I was being interviewed and I found this very distracting. I did my best to block out the music, and on reflection I should have asked for the music to be turned off but I thought I would appear difficult or demanding if I made this request. The questions were bizarre and often hard to understand. I had to ask for clarification and this seemed to cause frustration as they had to repeat questions and elaborate. I was interrupted several times during my answers. When I was talking, the people interviewing me were frowning and the atmosphere felt very tense and awkward.

An interview can be challenging and should be rigorous to ensure the best candidate is appointed. The purpose is to find the best possible candidate and so the stakes are high for everyone involved, but that does not mean it should be aggressive or designed to make candidates feel uncomfortable. The interview process should never be used to humiliate, embarrass or attack individuals.

At the end of the second interview, once I was alone, I cried. The questions felt unfair and often irrelevant. My confidence was shattered. I wasn't informed whether I was successful or not but I knew I did not want to work in a hostile environment that knocked my self-esteem and with school leaders whom I found to be very rude. I withdrew my application.

Fortunately, the first interview that I enjoyed led to a successful outcome as I was offered the position. That was a school where I thoroughly enjoyed working and it was a place I could thrive and flourish as both a classroom teacher and middle leader. Once I joined the school I read their interview policy which had a clear emphasis on representing the school in the best light and always being friendly, approachable and helpful in contrast to abrupt and rude. Remember, the interview process is not one sided and the candidate being interviewed has the choice to accept or reject the offer.

Interview with Jill Berry

Bio: Jill Berry taught for thirty years across six different schools in the UK, state and independent, and she taught adults to GCSE and A level in the evenings for several years. She was a head for the last ten years of her time in schools. Since 2010 she has completed a doctorate, researching the transition to headship and written a book about it: *Making the leap – Moving from Deputy to Head* (Crown House, 2016) and carried out an extensive range of leadership development work. She has given a TEDx presentation on the subject of 'Take a second look: Bring out the best in yourself and others' and she has published three short novels. Jill is an advocate for the opportunities presented by social media for networking and professional development, tweeting @JillBerry102 and blogging about education at https://jillberry102.blog/.

Below Jill Berry offers her advice to female educators to help them secure the right role.

Q1. When did you begin to take an interest in school leadership and why?

I began to take an interest in school leadership from my early days as a teacher. I'd look at others fulfilling different roles in my different schools (for example Head of Department), and find myself thinking, 'I might enjoy that'. Sometimes I thought, 'I reckon I could make a decent job of that', and sometimes even, 'I'd make a better job of that than they are doing'. That fuelled my ambition! I'd always rather be a leader than be led by someone I didn't think was doing it well.

Q2. What advice do you have for classroom teachers considering the next step to middle leadership?

Give yourself time to learn your craft – your whole career needs to be dedicated to being the best teacher you can be. But when you feel ready for the challenge of moving from supporting and constructively challenging young people to achieve all they can, to continuing to do that while at the same time working to get the best from the adults you work with, then go for it. It's exhilarating – and you will reach more students, and make more of a difference to their experience, by working with and through your colleagues.

Q3. What advice do you have for middle leaders considering the next step to senior leadership?

Again, you need to hone your leadership skills so that you grow and strengthen your skillset as a Middle Leader, learning from experience and resolving to keep moving forward in your practice, but when you get to the stage that you want to take what you have learnt leading your current domain and roll that out onto a whole-school canvas, recognise that can be thrilling and very satisfying. Show how you can scale up your current leadership talents and make an even greater impact as a Senior Leader.

Q4. What advice do you have for senior leaders considering the next step, to become a headteacher?

I found headship the best job of all – challenging, certainly, but extremely reward- ing, fulfilling and joyful. You need the self-belief to recognise you will continue to grow in the role; you can never be completely 'ready', and you will continue learning how to be a head from the experience of being a head. (Remember Robert Quinn's words: 'Build the bridge as you walk on it' (2004).) But it is well worthwhile – you will make a difference on a scale unlike anything you have ever known before.

Q5. Do you have any advice for the process of writing an application and CV?

You need to be honest, thoughtful and able to appreciate the perspective of the se- lection panel and not only see what you have to gain/how you can benefit. Explain what you will bring/give/offer/add/contribute to the role/school – use those words in the written application.

Q6. How can someone prepare for an upcoming opportunity and/or job interview?

My main advice is to put yourself in the position of the interview panel and antici- pate what YOU would want to ask to establish which of the candidates before you would be the most powerful match for the skills you need in the successful appoin- tee. Then think through/prepare/practise possible answers – and get someone to listen to you and ask follow-on questions and give you feedback. Go into the inter- view feeling confident that you have prepared and done the necessary thinking so that you will give carefully considered answers.

Q7. Do you have any advice for women that have been unsuccessful so far 'making the leap' and the transition to leadership?

Don't give up trying if you are committed to fulfilling a new role. Accept that if a school/head/governors don't choose you, then it ISN'T the right job/fit for you – the right job is still out there, but you will only find it if you keep looking! Listen to those who know you best and have faith in you (they know you far better than an external appointment panel) and let that fuel your self-belief. If you are unsuccessful in an internal selection process – where they obviously DO know you – then just see that you are ready for a change of context and a fresh challenge. Don't allow that to damage your confidence too badly and to set you back. Get a job elsewhere and prove how brilliant you can be!

Q8. What advice would you offer to someone wanting to follow a similar career path to yours?

I loved my career and feel very privileged to have had the professional opportunities I had, but I know I worked hard and was committed and tried to make the most of each one. My advice would be to pace yourself, don't be too impatient – it is definitely worth finding the right job in the right school at the right time – and never stop trying to strike a manageable, sustainable, reasonable balance between your professional responsibilities and your personal commitments. Being a teacher, and a leader, is an important, responsible job, but it is a JOB and not your whole life – it doesn't define who you are. Always remember that!

Q9. Why do you think it is important and necessary that more women are involved with school leadership?

Women make great leaders! It is such a waste of talent and potential if they aren't encouraged and supported to step up and to fulfil that potential. Lead in a way which is true to you – who you are and what you believe. Accept that you will make mistakes, but you will learn from them, and just resolve to do a little better tomorrow. Make the most of networks, including #WomenEd, #BAMEed, #LGBTed, #DisabilityEd and then pay it forward by supporting others. Leadership can be hugely satisfying and a source of joy. I want other women to experience that, as I did! Very best wishes to them all.

Thank you to Jill Berry for taking the time to answer my questions and contribute to this chapter sharing her thoughtful advice and wisdom.

Accepting the right role

It is a wonderful feeling when you have been successful at an interview. However, despite the successful application and interview this does not mean that the candidate has to accept the position. It is worth considering the overall application and interview process. Reflect on the communication, dialogue and overall experience. There could be something that was not quite right or something about the role had been revealed that was unknown prior to the application process. There is no obligation, pressure or responsibility to accept the role.

Candidates often forget that the interview process is a two-way street. The applicant is trying to impress and demonstrate that they are a right fit and the best candidate for the advertised position. However, the school and school leaders also need to communicate to applicants why that school environment and advertised role will benefit the applicant. It comes back to the key question: is this the right role for you?

Endnote

1 https://www.nfer.ac.uk/key-topics-expertise/school-workforce/teacher-recruitment-and-retention-in-england-data-dashboard.

2 Women in leadership

Education is a female dominated profession yet leadership and other high-profile positions in education are dominated by men. An article published by *Schools Week* magazine in April 2021 entitled, *'The emerging "super league" of academy trust CEO pay'*,[1] listed the highest paid academy chief executives. The wage varied and was dependent on a range of variables including location, number of schools and students on roll. In the list of the twenty highest paid bosses in Education in England, there was **only one woman on the list**. Despite the outrage the article received online, there were many people not shocked at the lack of female leadership in the list of highest earning leaders in education.

In March 2022, *Schools Week* published their annual CEO pay investigation and revealed *'a £15,000 pay gap between top-paid male and female leaders'*.[2] The 2022 article once again included the highest paid academy bosses and out of the twenty highest paid **only two women were included**. The highest paid CEO was Sir Dan Moynihan, Harris Academies at £445,000. Rebecca Boomer Clark, CEO of Academies Enterprise Trust was recorded as earning £285,000. This is not an example exclusive to education and the GPG is visible in global politics, business, sports, entertainment and many other fields.

In 2021 *Fortune* magazine published an article *'Meet the new Fortune 500 CEOs'*. In this list of 500 CEOs of the largest and most profitable companies in America, only forty-one women were included. Despite this shocking figure, previously in 2011 there were fifteen female chief executives and only two in 2000. The data do not lie or make excuses; the lack of female leadership is very visible.

Sheryl Sandberg, former Chief Operating Officer of Meta platforms, is an incredibly successful and influential female leader. Sandberg is a vocal advocate for encouraging more female leaders, she has stated, *'We need women at all levels, including the top, to change the dynamic, reshape the conversation, to make sure women's voices are heard and heeded, not overlooked and ignored'*.[3]

A *Schools Week* report exposed their findings about the lack of diversity in leadership roles in education. The article stated, *'Revealing a stark diversity gap in education's top jobs, our study suggests just two chief executives of the 72 academy*

DOI: 10.4324/9781003380528-3

trusts with 15 schools or more are black, Asian and minority ethnic (BAME)'. The report added, *'Meanwhile, nearly three quarters of the academy-trust bosses in our analysis were men. However at the 20 councils, more than half of the education-director posts were held by women'*.[4]

The DfE have funded and created the *Women Leading in Education: Regional Networks for women involved in education across England*. The aim of this project is to support the leadership development of women in education. The purpose of the regional networks, according to the official website, is to promote women in leadership by:

- supporting women with their career progression

- facilitating leadership development

- providing opportunities to network and share effective practice.

The website also adds, *'increasing the number of women in leadership positions is a government priority. These regional networks are part of our commitment to support schools to increase diversity in leadership'*.[5] There are local networks that aim to support and promote female leaders in education. The DfE states that the role of regional networks is to:

- raise the profile and importance of supporting women with their career within education

- identify and support more women with their career progression into leadership

- create local, regional and national networking opportunities to share experiences, such as job sharing and flexible working

- create the potential for development through coaching, mentoring and group discussions to raise aspirations and challenge myths and self-limiting beliefs

- work with other providers to maximise opportunities for women.

This is clearly a very positive and important initiative for aspiring and current female leaders in education.

Spotlight: WomenEd

WomenEd is a growing global grassroots movement that connects aspiring and existing women leaders in education. Through their books, conferences, online presence and campaigns, they aim to give a voice to female leaders in education. The WomenEd mission statement declares:

> Even though women dominate the workforce across all sectors of education, there are still gender and racial inequalities in terms of the numbers of women in

senior leadership, the large gender pay gap and the number of women who want to stay in education yet whose requests for flexible working are not met.[6]

The WomenEd mission statement adds:

Our mission is for more women in education to have the choice to progress on their leadership journey. To achieve this, we work to remove systemic and organisational barriers to such progress and to empower and enable women to achieve their next leadership step, if they choose to progress in leadership roles. Any income received by us, including royalties from our books, is used solely to run this website and other communication channels. No individuals or organisations directly profit from WomenEd.[7]

If you want to become involved with the WomenEd movement, I suggest visiting the website https://womened.org/ and following the social media channels to find out more. There are regional, national and international events organised by members of the WomenEd organisation, taking place online and in person. There are a wide range of written materials published from blogs to books. Subscribers will receive a regular newsletter with links to upcoming events, campaigns and further resources to support and empower women in education.

Applying for a leadership position in another school often comes with the challenge that involves applying against internal candidates. An internal candidate is not guaranteed a position, and whilst many schools employ internally, some prefer an outside applicant if they believe they are the best candidate.

There are challenges any leader faces when they are promoted. If promoted internally this will likely change the dynamics and relationships with colleagues. If securing a leadership position in a new school, it can be difficult to lead whilst trying to adapt to the school policies and systems in place. Other challenges include securing the position over a colleague or internal candidate where there can be possible anger and resentment.

Interview: Morgan Whitfield Carney

Bio: Morgan Whitfield Carney hails from Canada and holds degrees from Queen's University and the University of Guelph. Morgan is a dynamic senior leader, currently a Director of Teaching and Learning in Abu Dhabi, United Arab Emirates. She has worked for most of her career in British curriculum schools and has taken on roles such as Head of Sixth Form, Head of Humanities and Head of Scholars. She is known for galvanising academic enrichment, and her passion is teaching and learning.

The Senior Leadership Qualification Morgan achieved focused on metacognition and self-regulation initiatives. Her upcoming book on enrichment, equity and high-end challenge will be published in 2023. She tackles and reinvents traditional conceptions of gifted and talented programs in her upcoming book. Morgan can be found on Twitter @TeachMorgan.

Q1. Can you provide an overview of your teaching and leadership career thus far?

My leadership career has taken unexpected paths. It felt right to become a teacher as both my parents were educators. My mother was an incredibly impactful principal, and my father was a magical teacher who loved every day of his work. To this day, when I am introduced to people in my hometown, there is often a sudden intake of breath before a former student enthusiastically tells me how my Dad or Mom changed their lives. Entering education seemed like a natural step. This profession is powerful and caring. Pursuing leadership in education has allowed me to evolve, learn and find my voice.

I studied international development at university and trained as a geographer. I knew I wanted to work internationally and spent years travelling before earning my teaching degree. I'm Canadian with British roots, so I migrated to the UK to work. I began at a school in Birmingham, which was both a gauntlet and a trial by fire. It was also the best experience to start my career. Being in this challenging school taught me about the obstacles of teaching from every conceivable aspect. This forced me to constantly research, adapt, experiment, investigate and strive. From there, I played roulette with my resume. I considered schools in China and Kenya, then ended up in the United Arab Emirates (UAE). I meant to stay for one or two years, but instead made the UAE my home.

Over the past decade, I have had the opportunity to teach at outstanding schools and take on roles for which I am truly passionate. My love of academic enrichment has been the foundation for all my leadership roles – building programs with strategies to enhance the student experience in and out of the classroom. The extension and enrichment my school offered changed my life. I wanted to provide this to my students. I was a keen and annoying child who sat in the front row, peppered teachers with questions and then interrogated them whenever I missed a mark on a test. Academics did not come naturally to me, but I was earnest and eager. Independent study projects were my joy. The enrichment activities I was offered in school channelled this enthusiasm and shaped me. As an educator, my goal is to engage students who would otherwise go underchallenged. This led to designing larger interventions and programmes, my roles in leadership stemmed from this interest in creating extension strategies and enriching environments.

Q2. When did you begin to take an interest in school leadership and why?

Leadership roles at their heart are about empowerment. When I was offered oppor- tunities to build initiatives I jumped at them, taking on whole school projects with zeal. My first leadership role was Head of Department at a start-up school. This allowed me to shape the humanities department from the ground up. My future roles followed the same pattern, establishing new structures and systems, building teams, creating foundational policies and curating the curriculum map. As a Head of Scholars, I was given free rein to design the enrichment program of my choice. It was distributed leadership in action. I had an incredible headmaster who believed in hiring the best, trusting staff and not getting in their way.

Working under great leaders inspires staff to grow. I've worked with young ef- fervescent principals who operate with charm and zeal, and detail-oriented heads who develop every aspect of their school with rigour. I have worked under incredi- bly charismatic leaders, my favourite was uniquely able to unite a school under one vision. He is a transformational leader, who quietly and effectively builds start-up schools with the foundation they need to thrive. One headmaster I worked under has always said that he wanted his school to be known as a net exporter of talent. His school in Abu Dhabi makes staff development a priority, ensuring that staff are guided and financially supported through NPQs and MAs in Education. One of my favourite headmasters was a highly strategic leader. He was meticulous, analyti- cal, efficient, decisive. The highest compliment he gives is 'well that is immensely sensible!' Being sensible is indeed a key characteristic of leadership, and as charis- matic as all these gentlemen are, they are all very much substance over style.

I have been lucky to have these role models, and I've learned a lot from each. What is interesting, but not surprising, is that they are all men. This isn't unusual on the international circuit, where 69% of international school heads are male (CIS 2020).[8]

I worked with a female Head of Geography who is one of the most pragmatic, warm and incisive managers I've ever encountered. She shared her boundless en- ergy with her two small children. I am currently on a Secondary SLT with more women than men, and working under an intrepid female Vice Principal. She is known for her emotional intelligence. She is also insistent on being referred to as a Dr. I deeply respect this, as her engineering degree, MA and doctorate in education are what she wants the world to see first. This says a lot about how women are in leadership. There is a need to curate and present ourselves with care.

Q3. How did you find the application and interview process with leadership?

My experiences with application and interview processes have varied widely. I have had interviews that were free-flowing, fun, open-ended discussions with the heads of schools, debating pedagogy, going back and forth with ideas and evaluating where we sat with school priorities. These felt collaborative and informal. On the other end of the spectrum, I've gone through applications that encompassed full days of formal presentations, problem-solving tasks, data analysis, interview panels, tours with staff meet-and-greets, student-leader focus groups, one-on-one 'chats' with the headmaster and creating a video introduction for the boards of governors.

After being on the long-list, I once had to put together a full video presentation on my school vision. I worked on it for ten hours over a weekend and sent the link. The link was never viewed, but I was still short-listed. It made me question how much the school leaders cared and if the hoops were just for show. The culture of a school is on full display during the application process, it is illuminating and worth paying attention to.

I love interviews. So much is revealed in the questions a school chooses to ask including their priorities, their ethos and values. At the leadership level the interviewers tend to be very frank about what they see as their institution's weaknesses, and what the school needs to drive forward. The leadership team is who you would potentially be working with, so simply being in the room and interacting with them is a test of chemistry and synergy. No matter what the outcome, the process tends to be thought-provoking, it is a great exercise.

All that being said, the most intimidating leadership interviews have been the ones I've done while pregnant, the elephant in the room. I've had some nervous interviewers who delicately danced around the issue, it is difficult to address, especially on the international school circuit. The same labour protections do not apply. I'm not sure if the pressure I felt was self-induced, or judgement imagined, but the repercussions of hiring or promoting a pregnant person are real.

I also applied for jobs after taking a step down from a leadership position during Covid. The interviewers I had thereafter were quite frank about this interlude. I remember one bluntly starting the conversation with 'So let's get to it, why did you step down?' I could smoothly answer that during my 'break' from leadership I completed my NPQSL, presented regularly at conferences, secured a book deal and gave birth to my third child. However, I would honestly say that stepping down has been a liability that I have had to account for in every interview since. There is an implicit assumption that you couldn't handle leadership. Overcoming this hurdle, explaining and justifying my decision to step back from leadership, has led me to give this forthright advice to fellow women: do not go backwards if you have ambitions for leadership. It is very hard to get your career on track at the same level. Your best bet is to move laterally or redefine your current role.

The push for inclusive hiring practices is a challenge. A few years ago when I was on a panel shortlisting candidates, I commented that the selection looked homogenous, another member of the panel just laughed and blithely said, 'It's okay, nobody's watching'. I stuttered and shut up. It was a moment of reckoning. Establishing new terms for engagement is hard. When involved in the process now, I vet interview *questions, ensure assumptions are unpacked and aim for equity in the process. There is value in having diversity in schools and it is potent in leadership.*

Q4. Why is a senior leadership role rewarding and worth doing, and what advice would you offer to someone wanting to follow a similar career path to you?

Senior Leadership roles are only worth doing when they are the right roles. Leadership can often be seen as one-size-fits-all, when in fact it is about specialising and focusing on one aspect of educational development that you love. It is never simply climbing the greasy pole of middle leadership to get to the top. Being a senior leader is rewarding because you arrive at the role empowered and ready. Specialise and the reward is doing a job that you love.

I recently had a discussion with a dear friend who was looking for a leadership role that would allow her to develop curriculum. This limited the number of roles she was pursuing, but it meant that she would find the right role, one where she could grow and flourish. She found her passion for curriculum mapping after years of timetabling. These skills seem separate but are actually braided together. Leadership growth is like this, becoming more skilled and developing links between the various aspects of school management. I found this in my own journey when I first focused on enrichment and then branched out into co-curricular development, data tracking and reporting, and teaching and learning. There is the traditional academic versus pastoral divide. I began with an academic route as a Head of Humanities as a foundation. It was through my passion for enrichment that led to my role as a Head of Scholars and then Head of Sixth Form. My Sixth Form role was my first deep dive into pastoral management; to be honest I didn't enjoy the job but it did stretch me, it did prepare me.

I would argue that we are beyond a generalist approach to leadership development. If you are developing projects and initiatives that motivate you, then you pick up the competencies necessary for senior leadership. These include trust and the ability to follow-through, strategic planning, communication within teams, mitigation of risk, budget management, building of partnership, assessment and reporting, tracking interventions, policy writing, rigorous quality assurance and establishing ethos.

Q5. Do you have any advice about balancing a successful career alongside family life?

There is no feminist promise being fulfilled in school leadership. In short, I wouldn't do my job without a child carer to assist my family. I recognise my privilege, that I can pursue leadership because I have extra support at home. Even with the help, it is a battle and I struggle every day to be fully present for my three young children. I have done many a bath time with my laptop open, answered emails one-handed while rocking my babies to sleep, and missed my children's parents' evenings to prepare for an inspection. The guilt is omnipresent. I have the benefit of experience as a pregnant person and parent, it informs my decision-making at school.

The priority for a school is that teachers be effective and present in the class-room. Bogging them down with unrealistic workloads or ignoring their family, health and wellbeing will impact their teaching, and will hurt student outcomes. If we want students to have the best learning environment, we need the best working environment for staff.

Work life balance is often viewed as a sliding scale, where you have twenty-four hours of energy and you give nine hours a day to work. When in fact the two are in-terlaced, work intrudes on our family and vice versa. There is a temptation to ignore the simple fact, time is a lazy measurement. It is energy that matters and is finite.

In my role as a school leader I have changed how I discuss my family at work. Whenever I am at capacity I try not to mention my children. It is better to use quantifiable data, projects in the pipeline and an expanding remit. I think it can be interpreted as overwhelmed if you publicise that your six-month-old is undergoing a sleep regression. Discussing any obligation to your family reads differently when you identify as a woman in leadership. Family is often viewed as a limiting factor for women. I wish I was one of those effortlessly together mothers. The truth is that I struggle every day to give attention to my children while giving so much energy to my job. My self-imposed family gag order is not a recommendation, it is a survival strategy.

Often advice about balancing a family with work is interpreted as you asserting boundaries for yourself. The guidance is that women should speak louder, speak up and lean in. In this view, individuals are responsible for their own advancement and not accountable to solve larger organisational problems. The truth is that initi-ating systemic transformation is key. This means using your position as a leader to set good policy and culture in your school. It is worth mentioning that the protec-tions women have fought to have in other countries do not necessarily exist in in-ternational schools. Often women are not given easy access to labour laws in their language, and navigating human resources is a battle. Women can be at the mercy of an individual school's interpretation of the laws. Setting boundaries and having high standards for staff wellbeing is important. I have been vocal about relieving pregnant staff members of duties, giving them parking spaces closer to the school and ensuring that breastfeeding time is protected. I've done this because I've been lucky enough to have leaders do this for me.

One of the places I worked for went out of its way to provide new mothers with a lovely space to pump breast milk. The room included a sofa, fan, refrigerator and locking door. I knew this was something I wanted to see replicated in other schools. This also goes for a school creche for staff children, offering flexibility with hybrid or online meetings and enforcing clear email curfews. I've pumped milk in a lot of school closets. Depending on a compassionate or progressive leader to be a protector is risky. Kindness should be codified in policy, otherwise it is not ratified in practice.

While I believe I should be a proponent of fair conditions, having the necessary conversations are taxing. Social capital is burned when you are the person repeatedly pushing an agenda to move equity forward. Women and people of colour are often given the responsibility to fight for equity. This is exhausting. There is an emphasis on changing yourself as opposed to structures, processes and institutional culture. Women should just be heard, obvious needs for family care should be anticipated, and it is the job of managers, heads and governors to create the conditions for this to happen.

All school leaders should be wearing a new lens and promoting a holistic change in procedures, hiring, ethos and values. The onus should not be on individuals to advocate for change. It is a lot of energy for one person in an organisation to constantly confront the established norms. There is now a drive to put diversity, equity, and inclusion at the heart of a school's vision. Diversity drives innovation and better outcomes.

Being an outstanding school means starting with an organisational audit and doing the work. Not putting the onus on women and minorities to take on the labour of being heard, they should simply be heard because they are always invited into the room. Larger institutional shifts such as diversity tracking, feedback loops and transparency are vital. They remove barriers to who is at the table, cultivate trust and build psychological safety that can excel performance and foster a happy workplace. Tokenism and round robins for feedback don't cut it. These concerns are not necessarily amplified, or given credence or guarantee some accountability. We should not be going for diversity 'tick boxes'. Diversity is multifaceted and intersectional. While I've written about the challenges of women with children, I hope that isn't seen as having blinders to other marginalised groups (i.e., BAME, LGBTQI). For the most part, our (white) male cis colleagues aren't monsters. Microaggressions and mansplaining are not the main obstacles. Diversity is not a simple quota, it is building a culture. When educational leadership is not representative of the diversity of teachers or students in the system, it results in barriers and missed opportunities.

If schools want better leadership they need diverse teams. Dissenting voices matter. It is how we make better collective decisions. If schools want excellent structures, processes, culture, wellbeing and ethos, they need empowered women and minorities. Families and the school as a whole will benefit. Staff goodwill is precious and understanding from management reverberates throughout an institution. Retention will increase, reputation will rise, buy-in will become easier and the quality of work will be elevated when the balance and equity is seriously addressed through conscientious policy.

Q7. Why do you think it is important and necessary that more women are involved with school leadership?

It is 2023 and leadership should reflect the constituents. Studies have found that gender and racial diversity in the teaching workforce impact student outcomes. Our students should see the diversity in their classrooms reflected in school leadership. Women belong in leadership because leadership is better with women in it.

Q8. What are your future goals, aspirations and ambitions?

My future ambitions are to continually improve my teaching practice, conduct research, visit innovative schools, witness best practice, write books, share insights, debate with colleagues, learn from leaders, ask hard questions, push kind policies, investigate inequity, build strong programs and see students shine. Whole school leadership does not appeal to me, headships are hard. I don't want to spend my day putting out fires. I want to spend my years setting off fireworks.

Thank you to Morgan for sharing her interesting reflections and wealth of knowledge and experiences, offering advice as an international senior leader.

Leaders are always learning

There are challenges with leadership ranging from extra responsibility, often increased workload and difficult conversations. However, despite the challenges, leadership can be very rewarding and empowering. A range of skills are required to be a leader, and gaining leadership experience will likely enhance and improve these skills. There are financial rewards and benefits with a promoted position to leadership.

For many leaders the greatest pleasure is the ability to lead, support and empower others. Leaders have contact and involvement with students, staff and members of the wider school community. Leadership involves connections, relationships, working with others, championing and helping others. Leaders should never underestimate their role, significance and ability to make changes happen and have a positive impact on those around them.

Evidence Based Education published the School Environment and Leadership: Evidence Review in 2022. The review stated:

> Students' academic learning in schools is primarily determined by what classroom teachers do. However, there is good evidence that the professional environment in the school can also affect students' learning, in a range of ways. The responsibility for creating and maintaining the most conducive professional environment lies with school leaders.

This once again stresses the central importance and significance of leaders in a school environment.

We can constantly learn from other leaders, whether they are colleagues or line managers. We can reflect on their leadership and experience of being led by them. I have had the privilege to work alongside kind, hardworking and dedicated leaders. The leaders I enjoyed working with were approachable, willing to listen and showed they were decisive. I have also worked with other leaders that lacked empathy and did not model or promote a healthy balance between work and home life. It is very difficult to work with and for a difficult leader. I was still able to learn from leaders that I did not consider to be effective, I would ensure that I would not repeat their mistakes as a leader.

Spotlight: Sonia Thompson

Primary Headteacher and Director of St. Matthew's Church of England Research School in Birmingham, Sonia Thompson embodies many aspects of this book as she is a school leader, published author and she regularly delivers training and keynote presentations across the UK and beyond. Events she has spoken at include researchEd conferences in the UK and internationally, the online In Action Masterclass series and she was a keynote speaker at the Premier League Teaching and Learning Conference in Birmingham 2023. She has collaborated with many leading figures in education including Tom Sherrington and Ron Berger. Sonia is very active on social media and is a shining example of a female BAME leader smashing glass ceilings in different ways in the education sector. You can follow Sonia on Twitter @son1bun

---

Interview with Rachel Johnson

There is a wealth of leadership roles in education, outside of a school environment. The data available has illustrated men dominate high profile and high paid leadership positions but there are women driving education forwards in their roles. Dame Alison Peacock is the CEO of the Chartered College of Teaching, Professor Becky Francis is the CEO of the Education Endowment Foundation, and the current Chief Inspector with Ofsted is Amanda Spielman. Below is an interview with Rachel Johnson, former teacher turned CEO of PiXL sharing her reflections and guidance.

Bio: Rachel Johnson has been the CEO of PiXL since January 2020, leading a network of 2,500 schools from every area of education. The aim of PiXL is to work with school leaders to improve the life chances and outcomes of young people, an aim that Rachel is passionate about and totally committed to. She is the host of two podcasts, PiXL Pearls and The PiXL Leadership Book Club, both designed to encourage, support and challenge school leaders and to help find practical ideas that make a difference and positive impact. Rachel speaks at various educational events across the UK and is on Twitter @rachelpixl.

Q1. How did you become the CEO of PiXL, and can you tell us about your background prior to this role?

I became CEO of PiXL in January 2020 and was officially appointed three days after the death of my father who had founded PiXL out of the DfE's London Challenge in 2007. I had been in a number of roles in PiXL since September 2013 including being a Director and Head of Strategy. Prior to that I had been Head of English, a National Leader for English and Senior Leader in two great schools in the North East of England.

Q2. What do your day-to-day role and responsibilities as CEO involve?

Each day is very different! The key consistent ingredients are around people and direction. It is my job to make sure that the people on the PiXL staff, and the 190 consultants we work with, are equipped, energised and clear about what we are doing and why we are doing it and then ensure we have a shared understanding of how we will do it.

Everything is geared around ensuring that we are serving our schools brilliantly, listening to them and supporting them. We want to lead with humility, kindness, integrity and pursue excellence. I am always looking at whether we are all living that in reality and so I am in and out of meetings, listening to people to see if this is the case; we can't be talking about it on a stage if it is not the lived reality! I also meet commercial partners, other people in education who are trying to achieve great things and lots of school and MAT leaders on a weekly basis as well as planning and speaking at national conferences and other events too.

In terms of direction, I prefer Simon Sinek's term of 'Chief Visioning Officer', my role is to have the vision, communicate it, work out what might stop us achieving it and then removing barriers and creating opportunities for the change to happen. That is easily a full-time job in itself!

Q3. What are the highlights and aspects you enjoy most about your role?

I absolutely love PiXL and the work I am doing because I believe in the mission of it all. Marcus Buckingham talks about finding your 'red threads', the things that make you come alive, feel your best and then ensure that 20% of your day has those red threads in them. I am very fortunate that a lot more than 20% is a red thread for me in this job. I love creating vision and working out how we will get there.

I feel energised and inspired by speaking to school leaders about what it is they need and then be able to come up with content, resources and events that will make a difference to them. Content creation is one of my favourite things to do, this can be writing resources for staff and leaders, presentations of conferences, reflections on leadership, student material, leadership courses and podcasts. I feel the best version of myself when I am doing any of those things. To do all the above, I get to read widely and learn – another one of my red threads!

Q4. What are the main challenges you face or have faced?

Leading change is always challenging as well as exciting, and since 2020 I have gone through a lot of personal and professional change. My parents have both died in quick succession unexpectedly, my husband started his new Headship at the same time, and in January 2020 my children were very small at three, five and seven and then of course, there was a global pandemic to navigate!

During that time, I was also trying to work out who I wanted to be as a leader, what I believed I was here to do and how I could transition PiXL from one leader to another with change in the right places whilst strengthening the heart of it. I had to work out what my approach was, what my style of leadership was and be clear about the direction of travel whilst also ensuring that I was looking after the staff and our schools in that transition. I believe in Post Traumatic Growth, and from the very start of my tenure here, grieving for my father and starting a new leadership position, I knew I was in the right place, doing the right thing at the right time and growing as a result. One of the challenges is making the big calls and spending hours thinking and pondering about the implications of that decision, it's also one of the parts that I love though. For me, one of the challenges in light of everything above, is knowing what it is I need to retain balance and perspective so I can be at my best and serve others well . . . and to make sure I do those things often!

Q5. What are the benefits of working in education but outside of the classroom or school environment?

I am very fortunate to be in education and still working with leaders and students and being able to provide things that support leaders, reduce workload and help people feel less alone. One of the challenges I found when I was a leader in schools was that you don't feel you can pause to look over and out of your own circumstances, it is so easy to lose perspective and to only see what is in front of you. The role I have now seeks to create that opportunity for school leaders and to meet them regularly be it at conferences or with our associates, both approaches help people see the big picture, work out what they are doing and why, and then how to get 'unstuck'.

You get a very different perspective when not working in a school which can help you support and equip people in school. Ultimately, I never wanted to lose the impact I could have on students, and although this is a different way of getting that, I still believe it is something I am doing.

Q6. What are your future goals, aspirations and ambitions?

I am three years into being a CEO now and am still learning about leadership myself and how I can best serve others. We have a three- to five-year strategic plan around being unmissable, shaping leadership and speaking up and I want to be able to look back on this period of my life and be able to say that is what I did. For me, it is about legacy and ensuring that what we do now benefits schools now and in the future. I want to ensure that what we do at PiXL is unmissable because it gives leaders what they need so that they can be at their best. We talk about 'better future, brighter hope' for students and we have plans to create something which would aim to do exactly that which is in development and is very exciting.

Shaping leadership is something I am passionate about and have been since being a teenager. I believe it is important that we are deliberate and intentional about who we want to be and how we lead and that those leadership behaviours have absolute integrity. Speaking up is about being courageous, standing up for the things that I believe are right and speaking up about ways to change things that I think need to change.

Above all, I want to be able to say, whilst I am doing all of these things that these were the best days of my life. I don't want to look back in twenty years and say that, I want to feel that now and know it in the moment. Who knows what the future holds, but through the last three years I have learned that if I believe in something wholeheartedly and am making a difference, living in my 'red threads', growing and working on who I am as a leader and living consistently with the values that I talk about, then I am very likely to be fulfilled, energised and happy. That all being my lived reality, I have learned, is perhaps the greatest aspiration of all.

Q7. Why do you think it is important that more women are involved with leadership and innovation in education?

I think hearing from a range of voices is important in any sector but especially in education so we can represent the people we serve. I think it is important we have a range of voices around the table so we can get the best thinking from a group – different voices, differing perspectives and a chance to be heard and understood, and education is no different. That is how progress is made! I hear from so many women in leadership who say they struggle with finding their voice or say they are suffering from imposter syndrome.

I think many women feel like the underdog but what we know from Malcolm Gladwell's work is that often underdogs do very well because they are not really underdogs! We need to grasp that and soon! We may feel like we are the underdog because we are a woman in leadership, have small children, ill parents, complex family circumstances, competing pressures and are inexperienced in leadership

BUT those same things we think make us underdogs also make us compassion-
ate to the needs of others, understanding of other's family circumstances, efficient
because we don't have lots of time to waste, eager to learn and help us retain a
healthy dose of perspective. I think all human beings (apart from perhaps very
arrogant ones!) believe that they are the underdog in some areas of life. I think
that women have valuable insights that can help shape direction and approaches
to make a difference in education, and expressed alongside other views of other
people, may make the debate richer than it even is now.

Finally, some reassurance for those of you who are reading this book and who
are not in a leadership position yet. I never set out to 'smash glass ceilings', I set
out to make a difference in my classroom first and foremost. When others saw me
doing this, I was then given the chance to do this in my department, then across
the school, then across a number of schools and then, after several years in PiXL,
across a national organisation. It is step by step.

You may have ambitions to get to a point and break through and that is great
BUT remember, it starts small, it starts by making excellence a routine and decid-
ing who you want to be as a leader, now before you even are one. It is about becom-
ing the kind of leader who is worth following. It is also worth remembering that we
are trying to smash glass ceilings on behalf of those we serve who may feel like that
will never happen for them. This is not just about us, it is about how we can help
our young people grow up to believe they too can do brilliant things, whatever their
gender or background. If we can do that, then 'better future, brighter hope' will be
a reality not just a slogan. That is what I want more than anything.

Thank you to Rachel Johnson for her insightful responses and helpful guidance
for aspiring and current leaders in education.

Chapter 8 focuses on supporting and empowering women in education and
school leaders, at all levels, play a central and critical role in supporting the staff
they lead. Although offering support is part of the job description and duty of every
leader, leaders need support too. This support can come from colleagues, governors and the wider school community. Leaders are not immune to feeling isolated,
lonely, stressed and anxious. Support in a school environment should be provided
for all from student to Headteacher.

I was a governor on a school advisory board, not at a school where I taught at.
This was a fantastic leadership opportunity and I would recommend considering
or becoming a school governor. I particularly enjoyed this role as I could offer support, advice and honest feedback to the school Principal. I was also provided with
the opportunity to be involved with whole school decisions and gain insight into
decisions focused on finance, school improvement, inspection and more. Being a
governor is an important commitment, and meetings took place in evenings with
regular communication and required reading. This was a voluntary position and it
did add to my workload but despite the challenges I found it incredibly rewarding.

At the time of writing I have no desire to progress to headship, although my
feelings may change at a later date. Although I do not currently aspire to school

leadership, I do want to work in a school where there are female leaders at all levels. I am keen to work in an environment where women are visible, have a strong presence and are well respected. Every school should strive for this and ensure it is a reality.

There are many challenges facing the profession including funding, strike action and working conditions. The lack of female leadership in schools should not become drowned out by other important issues. This is a vital conversation but words are not enough, steps must be taken to promote women into leadership positions and retain female leaders. Collectively as a profession we must ensure the number of female leaders in education is a reflection of the women working in education.

Endnotes

1 https://schoolsweek.co.uk/the-emerging-super-league-of-academy-trust-ceo-pay/.
2 https://schoolsweek.co.uk/best-paid-trust-ceos-wages-rise-fastest-but-some-rein-in-pay/.
3 https://corporatetrainingmaterials.com/blogs/using-our-materials/internationals-womens-day.
4 https://schoolsweek.co.uk/revealed-the-lack-of-diversity-in-education-leadership-roles/.
5 https://www.gov.uk/guidance/women-leading-in-education-regional-networks.
6 https://womened.org/about-us.
7 https://womened.org/about-us.
8 https://www.cois.org/about-cis/perspectives-blog/blog-post/~board/perspectives-blog/post/head-of-school-salary-research-tells-a-new-story.

Reference

Coe, R., Kime, S., & Singleton, D. (2022). *School environment and leadership: Evidence review.*

3 Leading and delivering CPD

Everyone in education should be continually striving to improve and develop. Professor Rob Coe at Evidence Based Education has stated, *'A great teacher is one who is willing to do what it takes to be demonstrably more effective next year than this'*,[1] and the same principle applies to school leaders. Professor Becky Francis, CEO of the Education Endowment Foundation (EEF) has observed, *'There is a real appetite amongst teachers to hone their practice in order to consistently meet the needs of all of their pupils. In the aftermath of the partial school closures, effective professional development has never been more important'*.[2] Professional development is at the heart of the profession, as educators we have to lead by example and model a desire and willingness to embrace lifelong learning.

As school budgets tighten, more schools are looking to implement professional development that is low cost but can have a high impact on professional learning and pupil progress. That is not to say money isn't invested in continual professional development (CPD). Many schools recognise the importance of CPD and are willing to spend money on courses, speakers and other initiatives that can be helpful and impactful.

Every school contains a staff that will have different levels of expertise and different areas of interest. It is vital schools tap into this and find out the strengths and areas for development amongst their staff body. Internal CPD has many advantages, not just cost related. One clear advantage of internal CPD can be seen when the staff member leading the training or delivering a presentation knows the school context in a way an external visitor could not. This knowledge of the school culture, students, staff and resources available can be very valuable. Schools allowing members of staff, from classroom teachers to leaders at all levels, to deliver training shows trust as well as a recognition of their hard work, knowledge and experience. It can also provide a great platform for individuals to progress and develop a wide range of skills.

Many schools will embrace internal professional development but still also look externally for further support, guidance or inspiration. When precious money and

DOI: 10.4324/9781003380528-4

time are being invested in external CPD, it has to be relevant to the school priorities and areas for development. Quality assuring guest speakers or online courses can be difficult but it is possible and advisable. Word of mouth recommendations from other schools can be very helpful, but again it will be dependent on their context and professional learning needs. Senior leaders can spend time attending workshops or completing online courses, and if they believe these will benefit their staff, then this will also reduce the risk of wasted efforts, time and money.

The EEF published a report in 2021 entitled, Effective Professional Development. The EEF report defines professional development *as structured and facilitated activity for teachers intended to increase their teaching ability'*. This can be achieved through numerous methods and approaches.

The EEF report suggests *'School leaders should focus on the key mechanisms of effective professional development – such as goal setting, feedback or revisiting prior learning – when selecting or designing new training for teaching staff'*. This is useful for individuals leading and delivering CPD to be aware of. There are common pitfalls to be avoided when delivering CPD, therefore anyone who wishes to lead and deliver CPD should become familiar with the latest guidance and advice from research about effective professional development.

I regularly work with schools to deliver training as an external consultant or advisor. This work can vary from a 60- to 90-minute twilight session or a half or full day inset. This training also varies from online to in person. Schools may ask me to deliver a one-off session whereas others prefer ongoing training. As I have authored four books on the topic of Retrieval Practice, this tends to be the main area I am approached for to lead staff training and workshops. I am very happy and confident doing so, I thoroughly enjoy this too.

I have been asked to lead sessions for staff on subjects I do not consider to be an area of my expertise. Some would perhaps consider reading up on a topic and then delivering training but I do not do this. I would prefer to recommend someone else, someone I know will do a better job than I could. I want to feel confident in my subject knowledge and have a genuine enthusiasm for the topic I am presenting. During a question-an- answer session I want to be able to give credible, accurate and helpful responses. In terms of delivering CPD, it is much better to be a master than a 'Jack of all trades' because any lack of knowledge, experience and expertise can become very clear, very quickly to an audience.

An individual will likely have more than one area of interest and expertise. In addition to presenting on Retrieval Practice and memory, I also present on formative assessment strategies, professional learning and middle leadership. I recognise and celebrate my areas of strength and I am also well aware of my areas of weakness.

Senior leaders can be known for asking teachers to present on a topic that is new to them. This can be a good idea as it can give a staff member an area to focus on and learn but it is essential that time, support and resources are provided.

Asking someone to deliver a session on Cognitive Load Theory in the next week to colleagues, when that staff member lacks confidence and knowledge of the topic, will increase workload and likely add unnecessary pressure and stress. It would be much better to seek volunteers or ask staff members to present on a topic of their choice, one that they have developed and worked on and would benefit their colleagues.

Before I started speaking at events and supporting schools, I delivered CPD at the school where I worked. Initially this was very nerve wracking, especially as a young teacher and where most of my colleagues were more experienced, but they were very supportive. I was keen to volunteer with assisting or leading training. The more involved I became, the more comfortable I felt. This led me to work with colleagues outside of my department and be approached for help, support and advice on a whole school level despite the fact I wasn't a senior leader. I was viewed by my colleagues as someone with knowledge and interest in teaching and learning.

I would recommend that anyone wishing to deliver and lead CPD begin internally at their school. This doesn't have to be through public speaking and presenting. At my second school I worked as a classroom teacher without any leadership responsibility. On arrival I was very disappointed at the lack of professional learning opportunities available. I decided to take the initiative and asked the senior leadership team if I could create a monthly teaching and learning newsletter to share with staff.

The idea was discussed with enthusiasm and I was allowed to launch the monthly newsletter. I also encouraged other staff members to contribute to the newsletter with recommended reading or suggested strategies for the classroom. It was delivered electronically via email and copies were printed and available in the staffroom. I was very proud of this and grateful for the opportunity to promote professional learning. Despite not being in a leadership position, I contributed towards creating a culture of professional learning, dialogue and reflection.

Tips for delivering and leading CPD

- **Be aware of the 'curse of knowledge'.** Don't assume your colleagues or people you are working with possess the same knowledge and insight as you. Anyone delivering internal CPD will have knowledge of previous training so they can build on that and be aware of prior knowledge and understanding. There could be terms or acronyms that some colleagues may not be familiar with, so be prepared to explain or include information about their meaning in the resources used. In terms of an unknown audience, it is best to clarify key terms and concepts.

- **Reflect on previous training.** What have your colleagues responded well to? Has there been a session that was not well received? To both of those questions, consider why. You know your colleagues and have insight about what they will find helpful, useful and interesting. What are the school priorities and areas for development? As an external presenter, reflect on previous sessions and feedback to help ensure the content is relevant and helpful to others.

- **Be prepared.** Anyone delivering training, internally or externally should prepare thoroughly, it may be more relaxing to present in a familiar environment with familiar faces (however, some find presenting to their peers more daunting than presenting to strangers) but it is just as important to ensure you are thoroughly prepared. Ensure the passion and knowledge shines through.

- **Be aware of subject or year group specificity.** It can be very tempting to provide examples from your subject or year group/phase but try to gather a range of examples to demonstrate how the content you're sharing is applicable to all.

- **Combine evidence and experience.** CPD linked to teaching, learning, behaviour, pastoral or other elements that will impact pupil progress should be evidence informed. It is important to be specific and share the origin of the evidence in contrast to vague statements such as 'research says . . .' because audience members could quite rightly enquire; what research? How reliable and robust is the evidence? Was it carried out in classroom conditions or in a controlled environment? The more you know about the research you are discussing the better. Evidence from research is not enough, the application of the evidence is vital therefore it is useful to support evidence with real life classroom examples. Theory should be supported with practical advice and strategies. Combining both of these can add credibility to your content.

- **Encourage ongoing professional learning, discussion and reflection.** An external speaker may turn up at a school and present but never return, although it is possible to suggest and encourage next steps for staff. An internal speaker has the advantage to ensure the professional learning and dialogue continues. This can be done by recommending further reading such as blogs, research summaries or books. Time can be scheduled in the calendar to revisit the content or to discuss in departments before coming back together to reflect and share. Aim to do this in a way that illustrates how it will help staff improve and develop but be mindful of any additional tasks potentially increasing workload.

Interview with Kaley Macis-Riley

Bio: Kaley Macis-Riley is an experienced teacher and leader, and education consultant. She is fortunate enough to work in a school that serves the community in which she grew up, working as the Director for Curriculum Leadership, as well as some outside projects that she leads through her consultancy business HoDandHeart.

Prior to stepping into executive leadership, Kaley had worked as a middle and senior leader in previous schools within English and Literacy roles. Kaley has also co-authored two books: *Succeeding as an English teacher: The ultimate guide to teaching secondary English* (2021) and *Doing middle leadership right* (2022).

Q1. When did you begin to take an interest and get involved with leading and delivering CPD?

On maternity leave, I started to take an interest in CPD that was relevant and contextual; I read a lot about the principles of cognitive science, and it really piqued my interest. As I stepped into leadership roles, I found it incredibly rewarding to support other teachers with their own professional development, and to this day it remains one of my biggest passions.

Q2. How has leading and delivering professional learning for other teachers and schools helped you in your role?

We are always learning, aren't we? No matter how experienced you are, how many years you have on the clock, or what Ofsted or equivalent grading we have: we are essentially always 'requires improvement'. However, the education world has been victim to high stakes accountability and judgement for such a long time that it takes good leaders to truly gain trust that is the professional learning is the priority, with a focus on developmental not judgmental. Always. Once you climb over that hill, and colleagues see your role as one to develop others and not judge them, that's when the beauty of CPD unveils itself.

Q3. What are the main benefits and rewards for leading and delivering CPD?

As above, as well as helping others to truly be the best that they can be. As Andy Wolfe, the Executive Director of The Church of England Foundation for Educational Leadership says: 'When the adults flourish, the children flourish'. Nobody comes into education for the money or the ease despite what the mainstream media might have us believe. We do it because, as cliché as it is, we want to make a difference and enhance lives! Seeing the impact of CPD in the classroom, listening to it in discussions in the staff room, and witnessing a consistent, collegiate approach to CPD that is relevant and targeted to the context is a wonder to behold.

Q4. What are the main challenges you face by leading and delivering CPD?

Compared with my peers I am a young teacher and leader, and sometimes that is a little disconcerting to some. I totally appreciate many of the teachers I work with are old enough to have taught me English, in fact, one in my school did. But I do not claim to have all the answers, and I too am always learning.

Another barrier is often an understanding of the bigger picture; the why. Many people in education are used to working in silos, so a whole-school endeavour can often feel fruitless and 'done to' rather than 'done with'. Additionally, it would be amiss of me to not mention workload. Teaching is at its most cumbersome now and people are tired and burnt out often. CPD has to be a part of everything else and not a bolt-on.

Q5. What advice would you offer to someone wanting to follow a similar career path to you?

*Draw on your network of colleagues, even those you vehemently disagree with. You can **always** learn from them. Be humble and admit if you made the wrong decision. Never profess to knowing all the answers. Always draw on the professionals around you, be that in school, on social media, locally, nationally. But most of all, understand the why and know your intent thoroughly. Without purpose, what's the point?*

Q6. What are your future goals, aspirations and ambitions?

I'd love to be a head teacher one day, but right now I'm thoroughly enjoying my role and I think I will cruise here for a little while and take in the scenery.

Q7. Why do you think is it important and necessary that more women are involved with developing, leading and delivering CPD in education?

Who runs the world? . . . All jokes aside. Because (as Emma Watson alluded to) if not us, then who? If not now, when? Men dominate in every stratosphere of leadership. But we are a female dominated profession so it's time to strike at least a balance. Little girls out there need to see their female leaders in schools!

Thank you to Kaley for answering my questions and sharing her experiences, insights and thoughts.

Delivering external CPD and training

Schools often look for external advice and guidance, specifically in areas they have targeted as an area for development or improvement. If possible try to learn as much about the school or individuals attending your training. Context is key and this applies to professional development. It can be incredibly frustrating when presented information and advice is not relevant.

There are also differences across countries, with terminology used, government requirements and curriculum. A school in Wales will not need to know about the latest Ofsted guidance report as Estyn is the education and training inspectorate. The Teacher Induction Scheme (TIS) in Scotland is different to the Early Career

Framework (ECF) used in England. This insight, knowledge and understanding of context is a requirement.

Payment of consultants leading and delivering CPD is a grey area as there are no fixed rates. If delivering a one-hour Twilight session, do not think of payment in terms of an hourly rate because time will be spent preparing the session. It is highly likely the individual delivering professional development will have a secure knowledge base and experience they will be sharing with others. To gain expertise once again takes time and dedication.

If you are unsure about payment, speak to others in the field. Some people can be reluctant to share their rates but this can hold women back and contribute to the gender pay gap. Alternatively, ask schools what they have paid previously for external consultants and agencies delivering CPD. Some conferences may have a fixed rate for all speakers whereas other events will make a payment to meet the individual demands of speakers. The fee can vary, some individuals speak for free at events (often with expenses paid but this is not always guaranteed), others can charge up to hundreds or thousands of pounds. Value your knowledge, expertise, content and time.

Hosting a webinar/online event

The Covid-19 lockdown led to a rise in online presentation with people attending virtual live events from the comfort of their own home or viewing a recording at their convenience. Webinars can be profitable yet still offer good value for money for attendees. Setting up and hosting a webinar may appear daunting if it is new to you but it can be done with ease. There are fantastic websites that deal with event management and marketing, such as Eventbrite, that can help you launch your event.

You will also need access to a virtual video platform such as Zoom or Teams in order to host the webinar. It is often worth investing to upgrade your account to admit more participants and have access to different features and tools that can be used during your webinar. It is important to become familiar with the different functions and features, for example, muting all participants to avoid disruption and background noise during a presentation. Never share a webinar link publicly online as that can lead to 'Zoom bombers', uninvited guests joining and potentially causing disruption. The e-safety of you and your attendees is very important. Be prepared and ready to remove anyone from a webinar if their online behaviour or comments are inappropriate or disruptive.

The first point to consider before setting up, launching and marketing a webinar will be your content and focus. The webinar should build on your expertise, knowledge and areas of interest and also be of use and interest to others. This could be a timely webinar, based on the latest development, trend or update in education (for example, ChatGPT, artificial intelligence, has recently dominated headlines and people have seized the opportunity to host a webinar focusing on this hot topic). It is important to consider the intended audience; is it aimed at classroom teachers or school leaders or both? Is it for educators of primary, secondary, further education or all encompassing? Is it UK focused or open to an international audience?

Another important factor will be the date and timing of the webinar. It may be difficult during school hours for those working in a school to attend, although they may still purchase a ticket if a recording is made available. Mondays after school are often dedicated to after school meetings, either whole school or departmental. The webinar could be delivered as part of an after school training session but again this will depend on the relevance of the topic and target audience. Tuesdays, Wednesdays and Thursdays after school hours are more likely to attract ticket sales compared with Friday afternoons or evenings, or weekends when people are ready to relax. It is possible to host a weekend webinar but again it may clash with personal commitments and some people may naturally not wish to participate in professional learning at this time, whilst others find this preferable.

Eventbrite requires the user to set up an account before the user can access events workspace (it can be found via the section 'Manage my events'). Brief information is required such as a title and session summary. An image will need to be uploaded (select an image from a royalty free website such as Pixabay.com). The title should be clear and concise. Further details and description can be added below the title. Adding tag words to the information page can help Eventbrite market your event to the relevant audiences. Date and timing will need to be confirmed, and the option to host a single or recurring event is selected. If you are hosting an international event, ensure you are well aware of your audience time zones!

Once all the required information is uploaded, the event can be launched with a sign-up page to purchase tickets. Eventbrite will take care of ticket sales and communication with attendees. Eventbrite will send reminders to attendees, at intervals of two days, two hours before and ten minutes before the webinar. These intervals can be changed by the host in order to increase or reduce the amount of emails sent. The page will need to be promoted online to attract ticket sales. Eventbrite also offers marketing features to support the promoting of your event.

Advertising your event online should be carried out on a regular basis as social media users login at different times, and some more frequently than others. Don't rely on one method of social media, use a combination such as Twitter with Facebook or LinkedIn with Instagram. A hashtag can be created to promote your event and later used to provide feedback and share reflections.

Hosting a competition to win free tickets can help with promotion. Although this will cost the fee of tickets it can be worth it to promote the webinar and encourage those that did not win to go on to purchase a ticket. A competition can simply involve asking followers to retweet a promotional tweet, or to be entered in the prize draw or repost on LinkedIn. These tactics boost a marketing audience beyond your followers. Paid for advertising is another possibility and can be done through social media channels targeting specific users. The more money paid for the advert the wider the reach.

Another method of promotion is email marketing. If you have your own website and blog, you can send an email(s) to all your subscribers to inform them about the webinar and ask them to share with their colleagues. Ensure the email gets noticed and doesn't become drowned amid other emails. Make sure the subject line is promoting the 'exciting new webinar' you will be hosting, while the contents of the email can elaborate on providing details and a description. It is vital the email contains a visible link the reader can access to purchase tickets. Eventbrite Boost can help you run email campaigns and create branded emails to invite attendees to your event(s). The Eventbrite Organiser app can be downloaded so that ticket sales can be monitored to support promotion.

Although there will be cost involved (not for attendees or presenter if the event is free), it can be worth it for the support of a good ticketing platform service. Eventbrite offers a range of ticket selling options: they can recover a fee from the overall cost, this cost can be included in the fee for participants or can be covered by the event organiser. Participants can contact you via Eventbrite. This could include questions, feedback or for a refund. There are options to provide discounted ticket sales using a promo code or allow an option for free tickets to be assigned.

I would recommend asking a friend or colleague to act as a co-host during a webinar, attendees may arrive late and it can be distracting to have to allow guests to enter the webinar during a presentation. Another option is to pay someone, again a trusted friend, family member or colleague to act as a 'producer', responsible for allowing people to enter the webinar, control the recording and monitor the question and chat function so that the presenter can focus their attention on their presentation.

Ensure you host the webinar in a quiet space where there will be no interruptions. Wi-Fi must be reliable with sufficient internet speed and your laptop should be fully charged or have access to a charging port. If working at home or a school/office environment, it is worth posting a 'Quiet' or 'Do not disturb' sign to prevent disruption. Ensure mobile phones and devices are switched off or to 'do not disturb' mode. Make sure all laptop notifications are turned off and tabs are closed. Ensure a clear background, either a blank space or virtual background as cluttered can be distracting and look unprofessional.

A microphone can be a useful investment, especially if creating online content such as webinars, videos and podcasts. Most laptops have a built-in microphone and webcam, which is sufficient, but if you intend on delivering a series of webinars a web camera could be another worthwhile purchase. Lighting is also important. Position yourself with natural light if possible or ensure your working environment is well lit. Another purchase to consider is a laptop desk stand, providing elevation for your laptop and ensuring the presenter is observed is in a central position. All of these factors can make your webinar appear professional and run more smoothly.

A webinar can be interactive, especially with functions such as the chat box, breakout rooms, polls and other features. Allowing audience participation throughout is helpful to give the presenter a short break and encourages virtual networking opportunities. It is important to strike the right balance with interaction. Too much audience participation and interaction can take time away from the presenter sharing their content, and remember this is ultimately the reason why people signed up for the webinar. If the session is being recorded and not all attendees can see it live, then this is another reason to avoid too much interaction, as this will isolate those ticket holders unable to participate.

A great way to start a webinar is with a question. Asking participants their location allows a welcome to your attendees when they respond. This is a friendly way to welcome attendees. It can also be useful if you begin the webinar a few minutes early and are waiting for others to join. A hosting screen with the webinar title, your name and social media handles should be visible as attendees join. Be at your webinar early and begin promptly, don't wait for every last attendee to turn up, but instead show respect to the attendees that did arrive on time and begin promptly on schedule. There is more advice in Chapter 6 about public speaking and slide design and those principles should be applied when delivering an online presentation or webinar.

When rehearsing your webinar presentation, consider building in time for live questions, answers and discussion. Providing this opportunity can encourage more people to attend the event live in contrast to viewing the recording as this option will not provide the chance to ask the host questions. Question and answer time can be built in throughout the presentation after different segments but timings must be rigorous (for example, five minutes for questioning) to ensure the webinar finishes promptly. There can be opportunities for questions at the end of a session. Some presenters prefer this because it doesn't interrupt the flow of a presentation and if people wish to leave they can without missing any of the content.

One benefit of a webinar is the ability to pre-record the session or record a live session for attendees to view again or if they are unable to attend the original live webinar. To maintain access to the recording and ensure it is not used for other purposes (such as future training without seeking permission), I would recommend uploading the recording to a video platform such as Vimeo and YouTube, with an unlisted link (unlisted content is not available publicly or through a search function but can only be accessed with a specific link provided) to ensure only ticket holders will have access to the recording. The recording can also be taken down after 30 days or at a later date. It is also much easier to share a video link in contrast to uploading and sharing a large video file. This gives the host a level of control over the content they share.

Eventbrite and other event management websites can also be used to sell tickets for in person events and conferences. There are alternatives to Eventbrite such as PromoTix.com and Myevent.com. For further advice and support, there are YouTube tutorials that offer step by step guidance to assist in creating an event.

Delivering and leading professional development at events or working with other schools is certainly possible to do in addition to a full-time job (I know from experience!) but naturally it will increase workload. It will also be a good idea to inform your school about this. The school is likely to be supportive but there could be concerns or issues. You always represent the school you work for even when delivering professional development externally. Internationally many contracts do not allow employees to earn an additional income via tutoring or professional development, although a discussion and explanation may be enough to overcome this.

In addition to the extra workload, this will take up time, likely to be evenings and weekends. In my previous school the senior leadership team were happy for me to deliver external training to other schools and content for me to accept payment for this too. They advised me to manage my workload and not take on too much. There was one key rule I had to abide by; I was not allowed to request any time away from school hours to deliver external CPD, it all had to be completed outside of the contracted working hours. I thought this was fair as I did not want to miss lessons with my classes. I was living in Abu Dhabi at this point and the time difference (three or four hours ahead of the UK) was a big advantage for me as I was able to deliver online afternoon training to schools in the UK during my evenings without any disruption to my teaching time table and commitments, but it did take place during my personal time.

I reached a point where my workload was becoming unsustainable. I was Head of Department with a heavy teaching timetable. I was regularly writing books, blogs and articles for magazines, speaking at conferences and delivering professional development training online and in person. My priority was always my commitment to my students and classes. I made this clear to my publisher, editors and event organisers. However, I thoroughly enjoyed writing and leading professional development too. Before a breaking point was reached, I made the decision to leave the classroom to focus on writing and leading professional development with the aim to return to the classroom in the future. This remains my long-term goal.

Some people can sustain a balance between the classroom and other opportunities such as writing and delivering CPD but many will reach the point where it becomes too difficult. Options to ameliorate this include working part time or making the decision to leave the classroom and school environment. I made that decision after years of writing, speaking and working with schools. Those experiences enabled me to make the decision for two reasons. Firstly, I knew I would enjoy writing and leading professional development as I had already spent time doing so and found it incredibly rewarding. Secondly, I knew there was a demand for schools to work with me. This reduced the fears about leaving a secure and regular income.

Leading and delivering professional learning and development involves a lot more than standing up in front of staff and presenting. There is the burden of administrative work behind the scenes arranging and confirming dates and timings. There are the logistics of travel and accommodation arrangements (some schools and events may do this on your behalf but not always, and travel expenses can be added to costs). Invoices and self-assessment tax returns are other factors to consider, but support can be provided with an accountant or financial advisor. There is also the need to continually produce, promote and share your content to ensure that paid work is regular and consistent.

Building a profile

Building a profile and reputation is an important element of leading and delivering CPD (this is also discussed in Chapter 6). Event organisers will often want to enlist speakers they know will attract large audiences and this can be based on a range of factors. A profile within education can be achieved through the following:

- Being a well-known and experienced speaker on the education circuit

- Becoming a published author or well-known blogger/columnist

- Having a social media presence, with a large following and engagement

- Holding an important title or position in education

- Collaborating with other high-profile individuals in education.

For high profile individuals, these elements can be self-supporting. For example, a published author will use social media channels to promote their work, and as a result of being a published author their following can increase. It is likely anyone with a high profile in education will agree, it does not happen overnight.

Building a continually growing profile takes a lot of effort and time. Inevitably, there will be failures and setbacks too. Time should be set aside for social media, attending events, networking opportunities and so on. High profile individuals all have something in common: they share content. This content could be representative of their experience and advice, it could be through writing or public speaking or online material or it may be sharing strategies, discussing research or education policy. They all have something to offer. What content can you share? What can you offer to help others?

Delivering and leading CPD can be highly enjoyable and rewarding. Teachers have an impact on the students they work with in the classroom. When delivering and leading CPD to support other teachers and leaders in education then ultimately their students can benefit too. Therefore, supporting other professionals in education is to support learners outside of your own classroom or school environment.

Endnotes

1 Coe, R., Rauch, C.J., Kime, S., & Singleton, D. (2020). *The great teaching toolkit: Evidence review.* https://evidencebased.education/greatteaching-toolkit/.
2 https://educationendowmentfoundation.org.uk/news/eef-publishes-new-guidance-on-professional-development.

4 Innovation in education

Innovation is an exciting buzzword in education but what does it actually mean? The definition is open to interpretation but it is important to have a shared understanding of this term, especially in the context of education. Innovation is often associated with modern technologies and cutting-edge developments but this is a narrow view of innovation.

McKinsey (a global management consultancy firm) writes on their blog, *'In a business context, innovation is the ability to conceive, develop, deliver, and scale new products, services, processes, and business models for customers'*.[1] *Forbes* magazine attempted to answer this question in an article entitled, *'Back to basics: What is innovation?'* (December 2019). The article explains the challenges when trying to define innovation and how the term can become meaningless without a shared understanding of the concept. The *Forbes* article states, *'Innovation is something different that creates value'*, and adds, *'Innovation is not a one-size fits all term'*.[2]

These definitions and examples can be applied to business models designed for the education sector to help and support schools, leaders, teachers and/or students. Disruptive innovation refers to a new idea, concept or approach that reshapes or alters a practice or industry. Innovation is an umbrella term, especially in education. As professional development is evolving, the profession is becoming more evidence-informed, and as education continues to progress, innovation plays a role in these changes. In education, innovation often focuses on improving outcomes for students or offering ways to support schools which can be accomplished through a variety of creative and original ways.

Recruitment and retention of teachers in the classroom is a priority. However, many teachers are branching out to a side project (or 'side hustle') with additional professional projects. This can be great for professional development and networking. There can also potentially be an additional income. Women in education are taking advantage of the opportunities to share their skills, create new content and seize the chance to try something new and different.

 DOI: 10.4324/9781003380528-5

This chapter aims to shine a light on the women in education who have taken risks, demonstrated creativity and entrepreneurial skills. Innovation and enterprise can be challenging, often with many setbacks or competition but it can be highly rewarding and fulfilling.

Interview with Teacher Tapp:

Laura McInerney and Professor Becky Allen

Throughout this book I reference Teacher Tapp, as it collects and shares data from teachers. Teacher Tapp is a daily survey app for educators. The Teacher Tapp website states:

> *Teacher Tapp now has over 9,000 teachers answering research questions each day on the app. It's quick, easy and free for the teachers taking part. And the data helps make the media, government and education businesses sit up and listen to teachers.*[3]

Teacher Tapp was founded by two influential women in education, Laura McInerney and Professor Becky Allen alongside Alex Weatherall.

Bio: Laura McInerney and Professor Becky Allen are the co-founders of the daily survey platform, Teacher Tapp. Before becoming unlikely 'tech bros', Laura was the editor of *Schools Week* and Becky headed a research centre at the UCL Institute of Education. Both also trained as teachers and taught in secondary schools at the start of their careers; Laura as a citizenship teacher and Becky as an economics teacher.

Q1. Can you provide an overview of your career in education.

Both of us started our working lives outside of education. Becky worked for JP Morgan as an equity research analyst and Laura did KPMG's public sector consultancy graduate scheme. However, we both got itchy feet and moved into teaching as neither of us are very good at the formality and stuffiness of big organisations!

Becky completed a PGCE in 2002 at the Institute of Education (IOE), specialising in economics and business. Becky then spent a year in a school where she also taught maths, before returning to IOE to do a Master's, then a PhD, before getting an appointment as a Lecturer and eventually becoming a Professor. During her time as an academic, she spent a period of time setting up and running the FFT Education Datalab, which helped teachers and leaders make sense of how data is used within education.

Laura joined the teaching profession in 2006, so took advantage of what was then the reasonably new Teach First programme. She taught citizenship for two years in east London and then stayed four more years at another Teach First school before going back to her first one. In 2012 she took what she thought would be a temporary step out of school to do a Fulbright Scholarship studying education in the United States, but unexpectedly found herself in court over a Freedom of Information request she made to the Department of Education as part of her studies (she won eventually, but it did take four years and three legal battles!). After returning from the US she helped set-up Schools Week, becoming its editor shortly after launch.

Q2. When did you begin to consider taking on a new adventure outside of the classroom and what motivated you to do so?

In both our cases we were motivated to leave the classroom because of our curiosity and thirst for learning, and both of us fully intended to go back. Indeed, there's still time for that and we don't count out the possibility!

When it came to setting up Teacher Tapp a few things came together in a serendipitous way. Over the first year of Teacher Tapp we actually did it as a side project, along with our friend Alex Weatherall, a science teacher whom we'd met over the years at various events. The app goes off once a day at 3.30 p.m. and asks teachers a set of (usually) three questions. Laura would be at the newspaper, Becky would be in a research meeting, and Alex would be in school at that time, and if anything went wrong one of us would have to scramble to try to save it while the others were busy.

But we were also at particular moments in our lives which meant that its growing popularity gave us all a choice. Becky had two young children and was balancing the difficulties of school-age childcare alongside a lengthy commute into London each day. Laura hit a point where she felt that journalism wasn't the right career for her and she was also going through a divorce and a period of chronic illness.

Teacher Tapp was therefore that rare beast: an opportunity for us both to take our lives into our own hands, to build a thing we genuinely believed could (and has) change education research for the better, and would give us the chance to do it in working conditions that we could have more control over.

Q3. How did you initially find the process of setting up Teacher Tapp?

In many ways it's a good idea that we had no real idea what setting up a tech company involved. If we had, we might not have done it!

We had both worked in business, so had some grasp of accountancy and the rules, but we hadn't run a company before. Laura remembers going online to Companies House and filling in as many boxes as accurately as she could before a certificate popped out to say the company was set up! She then fell gravely ill a few days later and ended up in hospital with urosepsis, which meant she entirely missed the first few weeks!

Luckily, Becky had figured out how to get the app built in a few weeks, and for a very reasonable rate, via a tech whizz that she'd met at a conference some months earlier. As Laura was also bed-ridden for much of the next month or so, it gave her lots of time to come up with questions and ideas for marketing Teacher Tapp, which we then launched at the 2017 ResearchEd National Conference.

Looking back, it seems incredibly simple. We just did it! We literally designed logos and designs on scrap pieces of paper, we hooked up the tech in the most basic of ways, and our survey questions in the first few weeks were dreadful! We look back now and cringe.

But people got the concept from the off, and it flew. We had over 1,000 users very quickly, which was our big goal! At 1,000 we knew that people would be interested in our findings. Of course, now that we are at 9,000 users, we realise our naivety. And these days we'd like it to be many more!

Q4. What do you enjoy most about your current role with Teacher Tapp and what are the rewards?

Becky: Like many people who start new companies, I like building new things. I like the days when we have new ideas for how to improve our data and analytical infrastructure. I like working on what the app might look like in the future. I like thinking about how we can best expand to new countries, and putting together the business strategy to make it work. We're lucky we now have a great team to give us each the space to work on the things we most enjoy.

Laura: For me, the best days at Teacher Tapp are the ones where we get an unexpected finding that explodes a current myth. For example, when we were able to show how few teachers had CO_2 monitors despite the government constantly saying they had sent out huge numbers of them. There's nothing more rewarding than being able to set the record straight. That doesn't always make us a lot of friends. I remember when we found that teachers were largely in favour of the government's 'parent pledge' on English and maths – so many people were angry at us! But it's important that we share the reality on the ground, regardless of whether I personally agree with it or not.

Q5. What challenges do you experience?

Laura: I still regularly feel like I don't know what I'm doing and that I'm not a 'business person', although after five years I'm starting to accept that maybe I am. I also struggle with working out where to spend time for maximum effect. The same curiosity and impatience that has driven much of my career means I fall prey to focusing on things immediately in front of my face.

Becky: It is always hard to try to make sense of the market we operate in. We are quite a unique company, a sort-of community app and a sort-of survey company.

Our company must look in many directions at once, to serve teachers, schools and other companies working in education. It is hard for a small company to consistently maintain multiple focuses.

Q6. What advice would you offer to someone wanting to follow a similar career path to you?

Becky: *Be prepared to quit. A lot. Life is precious and we don't get much of it. Both Laura and I have accumulated skills through multiple industries. I've spent my life ignoring people who warn me not to quit jobs! Being a quitter is great in a start-up. You need to try lots of different ideas and strategies and be prepared to fail fast by dropping things that don't work in favour of things that work better.*

Laura: Find a Becky! (No, you can't have mine.) Much of my career has been completely random and I don't think there's a lot to learn from it in general, but working with smart people who enjoy the same problems as you is critical for motivation and success. At school it was people like my line manager, Sarah Greaves, and in journalism my boss, Shane Mann, who made all the difference.

Q7. What are your future goals, aspirations and ambitions?

Our big goal for Teacher Tapp is to make it the world's largest and most important research study of teachers. It's great that long-term studies like PISA and TIMMS have given such detailed information, but because they only happen every few years, they don't keep up with the speed at which the world changes. During the Covid-19 pandemic, we were the only country in the world that could accurately report what was happening with teaching because the Office for National Statistics used Teacher Tapp to keep a regular eye. How brilliant is that? Just think how different the world would be if every country could regularly take information from what's happening on the ground in schools and share it widely with policymakers. That's what we want to do.

Q8. Why do you think is it important that more women are involved with innovative enterprises in education?

Ultimately, the profession is heavily female-dominated, and any industry that doesn't adequately draw from practitioners in its innovations will end up creating daft products. So, if for no other reason, women should be more involved because they are often the people who have the classroom experience.

But also, just mathematically, the world is going to be a better place if half the population feels able to join in with the innovative enterprises being created. Especially when that half has been shown in study after study to build more stable businesses which grow slowly and are less likely to fold!

Thank you to Laura McInerney and Professor Becky Allen for their compelling responses and contribution to this book. If you are not currently a user of Teacher Tapp you can download the app via the Apple App Store or Google Play.

Launching a podcast

Podcasts have grown in popularity in recent years. The BBC reported on the growing emergence of podcasts writing, *'While podcasts have been around for a good decade and a half, they've emerged from their niche recently thanks to the proliferation of smartphones, podcast apps and voice-activated speakers in homes'.* The BBC report adds, *'Now there are more than 600,000 shows worldwide covering everything from sport, politics and music to the thoughts of geeks in their bedrooms'.*[4]

Podcasts have grown in popularity for several reasons, including the following:

- **Podcasts are very accessible.** They can be listened to via any smartphone or streamed online. There are podcast apps and services which enable the listener to discover a podcast of their choice with ease.

- **Podcasts are convenient.** They can be listened to at any time and any place. This may include going for a walk, driving a car, whilst taking public transport, cooking or relaxing at home.

- **The vast majority of podcasts are free.** Podcasters make their money from sponsors and advertisers, as well as patrons and donations. This offers a free form of entertainment for podcast listeners and subscribers.

- **There is a vast amount of choice with content.** Sport, true crime, wellbeing, travel, science-fiction . . . the choice can be overwhelming as there are podcasts available focusing on a wide range of topics and genres.

Many people in education have seized the opportunity to launch a podcast to discuss topical issues, offer advice on pedagogy and share reflections from the classroom or school leadership. Podcasts are a new and innovative source of professional learning. Teachers can listen to podcasts to stay up to date with the latest developments in education or gain ideas, insight and inspiration from others in this field.

Podcasting is similar to blogging, it may appear daunting or too technical to set up but it is relatively straight forward. There are various apps and websites that can help a user set up, record and launch a podcast. I use Anchor.fm but I would also recommend www.Podbean.com as I have used that with ease. That is likely a reason why so many podcasts have been launched, they aren't technically demanding or difficult. You can record a podcast via a smartphone or laptop. If you plan to interview guests for your podcast, you can upload a MP4 recording, from Zoom for example. You may wish to purchase a microphone for clearer quality of audio but this is not essential.

Tips to launch a podcast:

- **Branding.** Before recording any content consider the focus and brand of your podcast. Is it general teaching and learning or is it more specific to behaviour or leadership? Who are your target audience with listeners? Have a clear vision and use that to create the title of the podcast. An image or logo will be required to accompany your podcast, take care when using images to ensure there are no copyright issues.

- **Content.** Consider the content you wish to focus on, areas of strength and interest. A podcast can be a great way to share knowledge, experience and expertise.

- **Consider the workload implications of hosting a podcast.** Teaching is a demanding profession and launching a podcast will increase workload, but it can also bring personal and professional enjoyment and satisfaction. Time will be needed to plan the content of podcast episodes, in addition to the recording, editing and promotion.

- **Be consistent.** This is something I have struggled with. Initially I was recording podcasts on a regular basis but as I had other commitments the podcast became less of a priority.

Education is dominated by women, therefore women should be leading the conversation about education. A podcast is another platform for women to share, reflect, support others across the profession and feel empowered.

Interview with Impact Wales: Finola Wilson and Jane Miller

I completed my PGCE training in Wales and taught at a secondary school in North Wales from 2010–2016. During that time I discovered the company Impact Wales. Wales has its own curriculum and policies therefore it was fantastic to have evidence-informed resources relevant to Welsh education. Impact Wales continue to support schools across Wales with school improvement but they have expanded to work with teachers and leaders outside of Wales. Their online presence has grown and the content they share has become widely downloaded and celebrated.

Bio: Finola Wilson is company Director of Impact Wales. She's been in teaching, coaching and education since 1990 when she started her career teaching English in Greece. Since then, she's been a secondary English teacher, a Maths teacher, a school leader, an endurance coach, a personal trainer, a UK Athletics coach education tutor, and an ultra-marathon runner. She's also been a senior leader on the Welsh Government national implementation of the Literacy and Numeracy Framework and contributed to the writing of a national competency curriculum for schools across Abu Dhabi. As director of Impact Wales, Finola has created a free visual library for teachers based on the science of learning which has been accessed by teachers all over the world.

Bio: Jane Miller is also Company Director of Impact Wales. She's a former secondary Head of Mathematics and Assistant Headteacher with responsibility for assessment and progress. She started her teaching career in London in 1990 then moved back to South Wales. After being in the classroom for over twenty years, Jane was numeracy lead for the Welsh Government's National Support Programme across all schools in Wales. Jane is also a GCSE examiner, item author for national mathematics test programmes and has provided quality assurance and authoring services for international test series. Jane was also deputy programme lead for the national numerical reasoning marking across Wales.

Q1. Can you provide an overview of your teaching and leadership career thus far.

Fin: *I have had a very varied teaching and leadership career, due in part to the conflict so many women face when they become a mother. I spent much of my degree in English adamant that I wouldn't become a teacher. I believed the adage that 'those who can't teach' so felt it would be a cop out to become a teacher, how wrong I was! Straight after my degree I used TEFL (Teaching English as Foreign Language) as a way to explore the world and thoroughly enjoyed living and working abroad. After a brief foray into jobs in an art gallery and for Legal Aid, I completed my PGCE and started out as secondary English and Music teacher in a school on the Wirral, England.*

I then moved to be second in the department in English in a school in Swansea, Wales, which was a very different experience. It was from here that I left teaching for the first time to be with my sons. I returned to teaching as a supply teacher when my sons were getting towards the end of primary school. From there I went on to a full-time teaching position with a school in the Welsh valleys as a teacher of both English and Maths. In the twelve years I spent away from the classroom, I was able to build a business around being a mother and ran a successful business as an endurance coach, personal trainer, Wales's head coach for an all-female running club and a UK Athletics Coach Education Tutor. Leading the running club in Wales meant overseeing more than twenty running coaches and leaders as well as 350+ members. It was this additional career experience that gave me the confidence to attempt creating Impact Wales.

Jane: *I followed a very traditional route to leadership, studying A levels, off to university, PGCE and then straight back into the classroom as a teacher. Back in the '80s and '90s, being the only woman in a male dominated mathematics environment wasn't recognised as a challenge. It was just the way things were. I was fortunate to become a Head of Mathematics at quite an early stage in my teaching career and developed my leadership and management skills before the pressures of juggling two small children and a partner who was away for prolonged periods of time at sea became an issue. You quickly learn how to prioritise and work as efficiently as you can, but also how important your colleagues and* team are to ensure you are all heading in the same direction. Leading a large department with colleagues who ranged from many years of experience through to early career teachers was part of the job. My role in leadership was to recognise their strengths as well as know when more support and guidance was needed and provide it.

Q2. When did you begin to consider taking on a new adventure outside of the classroom and what motivated you to do so?

Fin: *I've managed to leave teaching twice. Once as I felt at the time, necessity as a young mother, which led me into a second career as a sports coach and coach education tutor. The second time because I was offered a role that was just too good to turn down. I'm so glad that I was able to be at home for my boys when they were little. By law there are always options to work part time when your children are young, but so often that option means you work long hours and squeeze parenting into whatever time is left. This wasn't right for me. In the school I left in Swansea, there were already three part-time members of the department, and I made the decision to do family and work life on my own terms.*

The second time I left teaching I was offered the opportunity to work on a Welsh Government contract to support schools across Wales with the implementation of the Literacy and Numeracy Framework. This meant working across forty-eight schools, supporting them to understand the new curriculum document, to embed it into their teaching and to help children to develop their literacy and numeracy skills. It was a fantastic job and one that I enjoyed immensely. Unfortunately, the Welsh Government ended the programme a year early and I was again at a career crossroads. It was then that I decided the best option was to continue the work that I had already started but to do it together with Jane under the banner of our company, Impact Wales.

Jane: *In 2012 my school was facing being merged with another local secondary. I was being offered a change in role and a whole new environment. It was this that prompted me to step out from my long-established comfort zone and try something different outside the classroom. Being on SLT meant that I was out of the classroom more and more, working with and supporting colleagues across the school, mentoring new curriculum leaders and leading whole school changes around national priorities in Wales. So, it felt like a natural progression to start working with schools across Wales as part of the Welsh Government's National Support Programme (NSP). It was an exciting prospect to now be able to keep my thinking and pedagogy as up to date as possible whilst working not only with secondary but primary schools as well. The shift from NSP to setting up as Impact Wales just seemed like the next step. Although I missed the interactions with pupils in the classroom, I realised that I was learning just as much from the colleagues. I now also had the opportunity to see teaching and learning at a national level and that makes you think and question at a much greater depth.*

Q3. How did you initially find the process of setting up a company?

Fin: *I've run two companies in my career. My first was an endurance coaching and training business, my second was Impact Wales. Jane and I talked about setting up a company four months before we actually did it. Jane was a little more reticent than I was. I'm very much the kind of person who agrees to do something and then worries about how to do it after the fact. I found setting up a business was straightforward, if a little daunting. We made good use of business support from the Welsh Government, and I taught myself how to use Twitter for education. We now have a Twitter following of more than 40k, our own Facebook group and a popular education podcast. As we'd both worked with many schools in our previous roles, connecting with potential customers was also relatively easy. What wasn't easy was moving from doing a little work for those people we already knew, to branching out to new schools and projects. Setting up a business is easy, making a success of it long term is much, much harder.*

    Jane: *Thankfully, Fin already had some experience of setting up a business. When you've been part of an institution for so many years, doing something different can seem daunting, particularly when you have family responsibilities and finances relying on a steady salary each month. At the outset, we identified what each of our strengths were and identified the things that needed to be done, allocating responsibilities accordingly. Hence Fin is everything relating to marketing and strategic development, I'm more organisation and finance. We play off each other's strengths.*

Q4. What do you enjoy most about your current role and what are the rewards?

Fin: *The most enjoyable element of being part of Impact Wales is knowing that we really are fulfilling our dream of making a difference to the children and teachers not just of Wales, but Scotland, England and further afield. Being able to look at an issue, consider the research or evidence for a decision, make a decision, and then put it into action within the hour, is amazing. I get to make the right things happen and that feels wonderful. We have the luxury of making decisions that align with our conscience because we are not ruled by a system or an organisation, we are free to do what we feel is right. Whilst Impact Wales is a commercial organisation, we are not in it for the money. The reward is both the freedom and the satisfaction that we are doing good in the world.*

    Jane: *No longer working with children every day, paradoxically has enabled me to make more of a difference. Having the time and space to read, develop ideas, deepen current knowledge and understanding is a real luxury. Time is what every teacher lacks, so being able to spend that time now delving into reading and learning I only scraped the surface of as a teacher is fantastic. Leaving the classroom has also enabled me to have more professional discussions with teachers but also with my business partner, Fin. I value that time to think and talk hugely.*

When you're running your own business, you never know what you're going to be asked to do next. Whilst some requests seem like a huge amount of work for just two people, being able to make decisions and then immediately be able to start work on them feels incredibly rewarding.

Q5. What challenges do you experience?

Fin: *Being an education consultant is not easy. We're described on a regular basis on social media as 'snake-oil purveyors' focused on making a quick buck, which of course couldn't be further from the truth. There's also very little camaraderie between consultants as we are competitors. The professional learning market is highly competitive. Not only are we competing with each other, but here in Wales we are competing with the free professional learning that is provided by publicly funded bodies such as local authorities and the regional consortia. Schools can access professional learning from regional consortia in similar areas, but pay nothing, so why would they pay for us?*

We've also experienced the challenge of protecting our own intellectual property. Once you're working in the commercial world it makes sense that what you make yourself is owned by you and cannot be taken or stolen by anyone else. Not everyone understands UK copyright law unfortunately. We've had to be incredibly proactive in following up every rival consultant, publicly funded official or organisation that's taken our intellectual property, removed our name and then claimed it as their own. It still happens at regular intervals. Our organisation is built on our ideas, and if people take those ideas from us, we're left with nothing.

Teachers and headteachers are also a really tough crowd, who demand that you prove your worth and with very good reason. The education of our children is not a job which can be bodged. So, everything that you do has to be of exceptionally high quality, it must work, and it has to be better than what is available for free. Another challenge we face is workload. I've had to learn to be tech savvy, to be comfortable recording podcasts and films, to create content that stretches my expertise and understand research and how it could be used in the classroom. The variety of our daily work is both fantastic but also incredibly challenging.

Jane: *For very many years I was on the inside, part of the establishment, fully accepted. Now, on occasion I feel that I am on the outside and that can feel quite lonely. We know we are in it for much more than just the money, but there's a common perception of the commercial world as being all about sales. It's challenging to explain sometimes, that we too have to make a living, have mortgages to pay, and that we can only give so much away for free. Unlike a lot of the public sector our reputation is everything. If we don't provide our schools with a good service or don't do a good job, it will directly affect how much work we get. Wales is a very small country. If you work in a school it can feel like everyone knows everyone else, so here, reputation is even more important. The challenge for us then becomes doing the very best for every single person we work with.*

The biggest challenge we've faced so far, has to be Covid. Back in March 2020, we watched our diary become empty. Sessions were postponed or cancelled and our future as a company looked very uncertain. Overseeing the finances when there was a real danger of there being no more money coming in, gave me sleepless nights.

Q6. What advice would you offer to someone wanting to follow a similar career path to you?

Fin: *Say yes to everything. Worry about how you'll do it later. You'll make mistakes, but each mistake will teach you something really useful. Don't be put off by other people's opinions of what you're doing, they're not the ones who have to make a success of it, you are.*

Jane: *Classroom experience counts. Bringing that experience into your new role will be crucial. That's not the only experience that you can bring from school though, especially if you've had a leadership role. So much of what teachers do these days is in addition to teaching, so understanding those tasks and pressures is crucial too.*

Q7. What are your future goals, aspirations and ambitions?

Fin*: We've managed to reach a lot of our dreams and goals already, such as providing support internationally, publishing a book, or being taken seriously by the Welsh Government! Goals are useful if they help you focus on what's important. I've realised it's not the size of the goal that's important, it's the value it has for you. My goal is to continue making a difference to schools, teachers and children for as long as I can, that the name Impact Wales is synonymous with high quality professional learning that works.*

Jane*: For our company, Impact Wales, to be synonymous with high quality.*

Q8. Why do you think is it important that more women are involved with innovative enterprises in education?

Fin: *As 51% of the population, and 75% of the teaching profession in the United Kingdom, women are still underrepresented in innovative enterprises in education. Even though numbers of women leading innovation in education may be strong, there is often a subtle but significant difference in the influence women and their male counterparts have in this sphere. Women are more often criticised and belittled, attacked on social media and are speakers at education events less often. Women put themselves forward less often for fear of being shot down and personally harangued.*

You only have to look at the response on social media to the few women in positions of significant power within education across the UK to see how difficult it is for us to feel safe to raise our voices. There is real power in numbers. A power that women need. We need the support and strength of other women to feel safe to innovate and speak out about new ways of doing things. This is why we need more women doing exciting and innovative things in education.

Jane: *It's important women who've already had many years of experience have a voice and get to share what we've learnt more widely. So often in education it's men with few or no family responsibilities who rise quickly up the career ladder, their single-minded focus and youth is valued more highly than experience. Getting things done when you have no other commitments is easy. Being innovative and forward thinking when you're balancing being in charge at work and home is no mean feat. We should be making use of women's hard-won experience and expertise, seeing their ability to succeed despite the huge additional pressures of juggling many responsibilities as the highest achievement. See the challenges of managing pregnancy, childcare and the menopause alongside a stressful work life as the heroism that it is.*

Diolch yn fawr iawn! Thank you very much to Finola Wilson and Jane Miller for their contribution. They can be found on Twitter, Instagram and Facebook @ ImpactWales.

An important note to finish this chapter is to reflect on how women in education can be innovative in the classroom. This can include using evidence-informed strategies to enhance teaching and learning or using digital tools to support lesson planning, design and delivery. Everyday teachers demonstrate their ability to connect with learners and pass on knowledge and develop the skills of the learners in their classroom.

Education continually evolves. Teachers had to drastically adapt during the Covid-19 pandemic. Teachers discovered innovative methods to support their students' wellbeing and academic progress whilst learners were outside of the classroom during lockdown. Teachers should be able to share innovative approaches or strategies they have created or adapted for their classroom. Teachers have always been resourceful and innovative and will continue to be, both inside and outside of the classroom.

Endnotes

1 https://www.mckinsey.com/featured-insights/mckinsey-explainers/what-is-innovation.
2 https://www.forbes.com/sites/forbesbusinesscouncil/2019/12/30/back-to-basics-what-is-innovation/.
3 https://teachertapp.co.uk/.
4 https://www.bbc.co.uk/news/business-46470428.

5 | Writing about education

Writing has become an unexpected passion and part of my life that brings me a lot of joy. Writing about education enables me to write about something that I have knowledge and enthusiasm for. There are many benefits to writing that include:

- An opportunity to reflect on your teaching and/or leadership practice
- A way to create and share content with an audience
- An outlet to express opinions and ideas
- An opportunity to be creative and innovative
- A way to become well known in a specific field or area
- A potential to earn additional income through payments and royalties
- Relaxing and enjoyable
- A way to encourage people to read more widely and conduct research
- A chance to develop a wide range of skills from time management to literacy
- An outlet to focus on your passion or areas of expertise
- A way to help secure a professional qualification.

There are many ways women can become involved in writing about education. This could begin, as I did, with creating a newsletter for staff and writing content to share with colleagues. Setting up a blog is not difficult and provides the blogger with flexibility to write based on their schedule and focus on what they wish to write about. Another possibility is writing for an educational magazine, this could include an opinion piece or an article focusing on a specific topic. Completing a qualification such as a Master's, Doctorate or NPQ will also involve a considerable amount of writing. Authoring or co-authoring a book is a wonderful achievement and is often the goal for aspiring writers.

DOI: 10.4324/9781003380528-6

Blogging

I began writing a school newsletter and after sharing ideas and resources on social media I was asked to write guest blogs for other bloggers to host on their website. After enjoying the opportunity to write blogs, which were often sharing classroom-based ideas, I then launched my own blog. For many years I enjoyed blogging and I went through phases of blogging frequently and infrequently. Blogging was dependent on various factors such as my workload and the academic calendar (as I mainly blogged during term time). In 2017 and 2018 I was nominated for the UK Blog Awards, as an individual entrant in the education category. I did not win but it was great to be nominated and recognised. I continue to blog, typically writing three posts per month, published on the website https://evidencebased.education/.

There are many benefits to writing blog posts:

- You can write about any topic of your choice; there is freedom and independence
- There is flexibility as there is no set word limit or deadline to follow
- You can write at a time that suits you and make blogging fit around your schedule
- Blogging can lead to building connections and a stronger network as people comment and provide feedback, embrace this dialogue!

To set up and launch a website for blog posts to be published is not as challenging as many people assume. There are a range of online tutorials and step-by-step instructions that provide clear guidance if you are unsure. There are plenty of hosting platforms such as wordpress.com, blogger.com and Wix. They are often free to host but you can pay for upgraded features such as a specific domain name.

Creating a website can be used for more than blogging. It can be a place to display testimonials and feedback if you have delivered professional development training or offered services to schools. A website can be the go-to place for people to learn more about you, your background and what you can offer. A website can be used to encourage people to contact you, either to provide feedback, ask questions or enquire about availability if they wish to work with you.

The majority of my requests as a consultant offering professional development presentations and workshops have been received through the contact page on my website (this is followed by requests via social media). The requests through my website are directed to my email address therefore I can send a direct reply. If you are serious about writing and/or branching out to deliver professional training, then it is worth investing time and money to create a professional, slick and easy to navigate website.

When creating a website it is important to create a unique domain, one that is available. This can include your name or the title of your blog. My first book was entitled *Love to teach: Research and resources for every classroom* (2018) and I also launched my own podcast entitled: *The love to teach podcast.* Therefore, it made sense for me to include Love To Teach in my website domain name. That name was taken so I selected www.lovetoteach87.com and although this is relevant to my work, my content has now evolved and I am considering a rebranding and redesign of my website. It is important to keep a domain name quite simple and memorable. The domain name should include something about you or the content you share, so that it is relevant and can help attract an audience.

Once you have set up your blog and you are happy with the layout, design and are confident in how to navigate and use the website (this includes uploading content and being able to review statistical data about engagement), then you can write and publish a blog post. Below are my tips for writing blog posts:

- **Read lots of other blogs in the field of education.** Observe their writing style, approach, structure, word count and tone. This will be very insightful and helpful. There are lots of classroom-based bloggers, regularly writing about their classroom experiences, it is worth reading a wide range of these blog posts.

- **Know your stuff.** Pick a topic to write about where you have expertise or interest and don't be afraid to let that shine through. It can be useful to provide the reader with some context as to why you are writing that specific blog post.

- **Be mindful of wordcount.** Although blogging doesn't have the restrictions of word limits and deadlines, it is still important to get the balance right with the word count. If the blog is too brief then it can lack substance or supporting details that can strengthen the post. If it is too lengthy readers may not reach the end, as blog posts are intended to be short reads in comparison to an essay or book. If your blog is very lengthy consider splitting the overall posts into a series of blog posts focusing on the topic with part one and part two. A suggested word count would be 600–800 words.

- **Keep the tone professional yet informal.** Blogging is not like writing for a qualification or essay. The tone can be lighter and conversational.

- **Double check.** Before hitting publish, ask others to read your blog and provide feedback or self-check and correct your first draft. Others can provide feedback on literacy and grammar, as errors are easily made, therefore self-checking and proofing is very important. A trusted friend or colleague can offer feedback about the content too.

- **Be aware of the 'curse of knowledge'**, (this is mentioned again in the next chapter). The 'curse of knowledge' is a cognitive bias where we assume others possess the knowledge we have. If using key terms and acronyms do not assume everyone in education will be familiar with these, especially as acronyms vary across schools and counties or countries. A blog can reach an international audience so it is important to keep that in mind when writing.

- **Credit where appropriate**. Aim to include references, this makes points and arguments appear more credible in contrast to making sweeping statements without any evidence. It is important to credit others when quoting their work or sharing their content, this can include hyperlinks to the original material and links for further reading.

- **Consider structure**. Use headings and subheadings to help structure your content and make sure key points and arguments stand out clearly. Bullet points can be used as an effective way to offer tips, advice or break down a topic into concise points.

- **Wrap it up!** Although a formal conclusion is not necessary with a blog post, a short summary at the end is a great way to wrap up the contents of your blog post.

Writing a blog post will not guarantee people will see the blog or read it and that is the aim of blogging. Bloggers often rely on social media platforms to share their content to their followers and will ask others to share with their followers too. I have always believed that blogging and social media in education naturally complement and support each other. Social media can be a great way to share blog posts, and through sharing regular content and blogs on social media, it is likely to lead to increase in followers and engagement on social media.

Women can struggle with self-promotion and sharing their work, content or achievements. Imposter syndrome may kick in and cause doubt or panic, but it is important to remember that we all have something worth saying and sharing. A classroom teacher reflecting on their daily practice is not only a useful method of reflection but it will often be of interest and help to other teachers.

Self-promoting and sharing a blog post needs to be done on a regular basis and across a range of social media platforms to reach a wider audience. It is important to remember that building a successful blog, with wider readership and subscribers, can take a long time. Patience, resilience and consistency with blogging will often lead to great results. Once you have subscribers they will then receive all blog posts through email communication as that is what they have signed up for.

Another challenge with blogging (and this is relevant to any form of publishing including writing for a magazine or authoring a book) can be negative and critical feedback. Debate and discussion can be healthy but the reality is some feedback online is not always professional or kind. I have received comments that were unexpected, unpleasant and made me reconsider writing as I wasn't comfortable with confrontation.

I have developed more resilience as a writer. I will engage with questions and feedback but I have the choice to ignore and sometimes I do that. Any writer that is publishing content is putting themselves in a position open to critique. A writer must take the rough with the smooth, it isn't always praise, likes and retweets. Unless writing about deliberately controversial topics and sharing extreme opinions, it is unlikely that a backlash will occur or be a regular occurrence. Any negativity can be outweighed by the benefits that writing can bring.

Writing for magazines

After gaining experience as a blogger, I began writing articles for various magazines. During my time teaching and living in Abu Dhabi I became a regular columnist for *Education Journal Middle East* and also contributed articles to *Teach Middle East Magazine.* In 2020 I became a regular writer for *TES* (Times Education Supplement) and *TES International.* My articles have been featured online and in the printed publication. The TES articles vary from writing about teaching in an international context, teaching and learning strategies, professional development, and I was very pleased I was able to write about the challenges I face as a classroom teacher with hearing loss. I have also written for *UKEd* magazine, *Innovate My School, HWRK* magazine, and I have further aspirations with my writing too.

There are several reasons why writing articles can be preferable to blogging. Firstly, published articles often (not always) involve a payment. The fee can vary from £50 to £250 depending on the publication and whether it is online or print. A blog, unless a blogger branches out to allow advertising and sponsors, does not have the same financial incentive or reward.

Another reason some may prefer writing articles for magazines in contrast to blogging is because there is the support from an editor. My editor at *TES* is Dan Worth, whom I really enjoy working with because he will often send me back my article that contains the core key messages but he has changed the structure and often made the content clearer and concise. A good editor will not overhaul an article but will make an improvement and have a sharp eye recognising any typing errors or mistakes.

A key point to consider when reflecting on blogging versus writing for an educational magazine, there is often a larger audience for a magazine article in contrast to blogging. An established and well-known magazine will have a solid reader base. This enables the writer to share their content with a wider audience and the magazine will also promote the article widely. It can take a lot of effort, time and self-promotion to share a blog widely.

The potential frustrations or challenges with writing articles for a magazine, in contrast to blogging, is that there are often criteria and guidance to follow. There will likely be a word count, this can vary from 600 to 1200 words. An editor may cut content or even reject an idea if they do not think that it is relevant, interesting or will attract readers. There can be a time delay between writing content and the publication, this can be due to a schedule of other articles, whereas a blog can be shared when the blogger wishes to. Reaching a wider audience via a magazine can be great but it can also lead to more criticism and negative feedback, especially if the focus of the article is considered controversial.

Interview with Leisa Grace

Bio: Leisa Grace is the Editorial Director of *Teach Middle East*. She has been working in education for over twenty-two years as a teacher, Head of Department, Education Advisor and School Leader. Leisa Grace has worked in the United Kingdom and the United Arab Emirates. She enjoys sharing her passion for education through her speaking, writing and editing. Leisa is the host of the Teach Middle East Podcast and the founder of the *Education Roundup Middle East*, a weekly newsletter sharing highlights and insights on education in the Middle East.

She is active on social media @leisagrace on Twitter; Facebook: https://www.facebook.com/TeachMiddleEastMagazine/; LinkedIn: https://www.linkedin.com/in/leisagrace/; and Instagram: https://www.instagram.com/teachmiddleeast/.

Q1. Can you tell us why and how you made the transition from a teacher and school leader to editor and podcaster?

I have always enjoyed writing. I am a former teacher of Modern Languages. I always blogged and wrote articles as a hobby. After having my children, I found that being a school leader was really taxing, and I was not able to spend as much time with them as I wanted, so I started to look at alternative ways of staying in Education while being present for my kids. This is when I started to take writing more seriously. Writing and editing for Teach Middle East *allow me to be able to work around my children's schedule. I also am able to work a lot more from home, which means that I can drop them to school and pick them up.*

Podcasting fell into my lap. My colleagues suggested that I start a podcast, and I resisted for a long time, but once I got going, I quickly realised that I loved it. It has allowed me to talk with some amazing people whom I would not have been able to speak with ordinarily. It turns out that I love to chat. I always thought I was quite reserved, and I still am, but as soon as I get on the podcast, I can talk for hours nonstop, especially if the conversation is interesting. I have now become a podcast fan. Forget Netflix, now I binge listen to podcasts.

Q2. Can you tell us about what your current role involves as editorial director of an international magazine?

In my role as Editorial Director of Teach Middle East, *I work with my team to come up with the themes of each issue of the magazine. I do research and write articles for educators on various topics. I also collect and copyedit articles from contributors. My role also involves planning training events and conferences for educators and school leaders.*

I also host the Teach Middle East Podcast. In doing so, I write the questions and coordinate with the guests. Thankfully we have a podcast editor who takes care of all of the editing!

Q3. What are the main rewards and benefits of your current role?

The main reward of my role is that I am still in Education. I love education, and although I wanted a change from being school based, I did not want to stray far from education, and this role has allowed me to keep my fingers firmly in the education pie.

Another key benefit of the role is that I get to meet and learn from some amazing people. If I was school based, I would not have the flexibility I do to attend and host various events. I am also often called on to speak and comment on various things that are happening in the field. You cannot beat that.

Q4. What are the main challenges you have experienced during your career in education?

When I was a school leader, the hours were brutal. I would leave school late and still come home and work. There was very little flexibility, and with young children or a family, that can be really hard. In fact, it can be hard on anyone. I also did not enjoy the rapid changes that happen in education. Policies and programmes are not normally given enough time to be embedded properly.

I also disliked being dictated to by policy makers who were out of touch with what is happening in schools and classrooms on a daily basis. The politicisation of education is a real bugbear of mine.

Q5. You often encourage others in education to create and share content. Why do you think this is important?

Content gives you a voice. It allows you to share your expertise and make a contribution to the field. Everyone has something valuable to share. It is only when we share content that others will benefit from the knowledge that we have. Creating content has been given a bad rap recently because of all these so called 'influencers', but educators counter this by sharing valuable content for their colleagues and wider society. All voices matter.

Q6. Can you offer any advice for women in education that wish to write an article and secure publication in an educational magazine?

My first advice is to decide what you are passionate about. What could you write or talk about at the drop of a hat? Once you know this, then start to send pitches to publications. If you pitch once and do not hear back, do not give up, pitch again and again. Do not be afraid to try. The reason many men are published is not that they know more than us, the difference is that they are not scared to put themselves forward. Come on, women, we are smart and capable; let the world know by stepping forward.

Q7. What advice would you offer to someone wanting to follow a similar career path to you?

My career path was a bit winding, but eventually it led me back to what I enjoy doing most, which is writing. It may sound cliché and fluffy, but I say find out what you enjoy doing and pursue that. It does not mean that you won't have days that you will not hate it, but if you love it a lot more than you hate it, then you are on the right path.

The other thing is that you might have to do it for free for a long time before you start getting paid for it. In those days, do not be discouraged, just keep going and eventually it will start paying.

Q8. What are your future goals, aspirations and ambitions?

My goal is to double down on content creation. I am in the midst of starting a personal YouTube channel, something I have always wanted to do. I also want to do more events and work in countries like Qatar and Saudi Arabia. Apart from that I just want to make sure I am there for my kids as they transition into secondary school and beyond. I will still be podcasting and writing for Teach Middle East.

Q9. You have organised one of the leading educational conferences in the Middle East. How do you ensure a diverse range of speakers at your events?

I love planning the speaker line-up for conferences. When I am working with the team on this, I focus on making sure that a diverse range of voices are being amplified. I am deliberate in seeking out voices from under represented communities. Conferences are more valuable when the presenters are as diverse as possible but conference organisers have to be intentional about ensuring diversity. You cannot sit and wait for the right mix of people to apply to speak; you have to go out and seek them and invite them to present.

Q10. Why do you think it is important and necessary that more women are writing about education?

Women have the ability to see the bigger picture more easily, and they are also able to care for and nurture people. Education is a people business, and our ability as women to take care of people means that we need to write and lend our voices more often to the discussion. If we do not write and share, then we become complicit with what is happening. Sometimes the only weapon we have is our pen (keyboard) to fight against what we think is not right in the field.

Thank you to Leisa Grace for sharing her unique and insightful experiences and advice as editor, content creator and podcast host.

Authoring a book

Most authors that I know in the field of education had a similar path to me, which involved writing blog posts and/or articles before progressing to writing a book of their own. Although the style differs greatly between blogging, articles and authoring a book I do believe gaining experience as a writer to be an essential step towards becoming a published author. It is possible to become an author without writing blogs and articles but spending time writing can help you to develop your style and gain experience with research, reflection and self-checking and correcting.

Several people in education have told me they want to write a book. In response I ask: what do you want to write about? I am surprised how common the answer is: they don't know. The starting point has to be what do you want to write about? Only then can you think about the next steps such as securing a publisher or deciding to self-publish.

The content of a book is key. Focus on an area in which you are invested. Writing a book is a labour of love, with a huge amount of time, effort and energy dedicated to the process. That time and commitment should be spent on a topic/area you believe is important and others should read about.

It is possible to write your book and then find a publisher but I would not advise this. Publishers will ask potential authors to complete an author questionnaire or review. This will include a range of questions about you, your professional background and why you have the expertise and ability to write the book. Other questions will focus on the content of the book, this process does vary with different publishers. If you write a manuscript prior to completing the author application, you may need to radically change your original manuscript. The publisher may suggest a different title and shift in focus and they may set a strict word count.

The publisher will be considering if there are any books published already that focus on the same content, therefore it has already been covered. The publisher will want to know who the intended target audience is, is it a niche and specific audience or is it a wider and more general audience? How does the concept of the book stand out and why is it original? Is it timely or is it something that has lost its relevance or could potentially have a short shelf life? Securing a publisher can be a life changing experience, therefore this is not something to be rushed.

If one publisher rejects an idea, then contact another publisher! There is also the option to self-publish and this will guarantee your book is published and available to buy. There are several pros and cons to consider with self-publishing versus securing a contract with a publishing house.

The advantages of self-publishing include complete control and autonomy with content, word count and deadlines. Self-publishing provides the author with greater independence and freedom. Self-publishing will also result in higher royalties in comparison to publishing houses (but this is dependent on sales figures). Publishing houses provide authors with a royalty payment based on a percentage of overall sales. This can vary with publishers and be dependent on a range of factors such as the experience and profile of the author. The percentage can vary (based on a wide range of factors) and if co-authoring a book royalties can be divided.

There are disadvantages of self-publishing. The support of publishing houses with an editorial and graphic design team will be absent. Publishers can also offer support with promotion and marketing. This often results in the self-published author spending more time investing in self-promotion, and the overall success of promotion and sales can depend on the following and connections of the author.

Interview with Haili Hughes

Bio: Haili Hughes is Head of Education at IRIS Connect and Principal Lecturer in professional development and mentoring at the University of Sunderland in England. She is also a former English teacher, Head of Department and Senior Leader. She has completed three Master's degrees and is now completing a Doctorate in Education. Haili is passionate about attracting English teachers into the profession and encouraging students to study English in Further Education (FE) and Higher Education (HE).

In addition to delivering CPD across the world, Haili also delivers workshops in schools across the UK, with the most able learners, particularly those from disadvantaged backgrounds, to raise aspirations and training staff to ensure that they are challenging pupils and developing their pedagogy to meet their needs. In her spare time, she has written three education books and is currently writing the fourth and fifth for established education publishers, as well as writing for the *TES* and other publications.

Q1. When did you begin writing about education?

From being a small child, I had always wanted to be a writer and I was lucky enough to achieve my dream, in a journalistic sense, when I was appointed as a graduate trainee at a prestigious national newspaper journalist at 21. It was an incredible, but challenging, experience and I loved the buzz of seeing my own name in print every Sunday. As someone from a very working-class background, I was the first person in my family to go to university and the day I got my first splash (newspaper front page) it felt like a dream world. I couldn't believe it to be honest!

Like many dreams, I woke up and after my newspaper was closed for phone hacking, I had to retrain and choose another career and with an English degree, the natural choice was teaching. I spent the next decade teaching and absolutely loved it. With my journalistic experience and acumen, I attempted to write for TES and other education publications a few times, but never received an email reply. So alongside teaching, I became the deputy editor of a very successful glossy, vintage magazine and gave up on the education writing.

Then in 2018, after ten years of infertility and recurrent miscarriages, I was blessed to give birth to my daughter and suddenly found myself on maternity leave and a little bit bored. I spent lots of time attending baby groups, but I also felt my mind was turning to mush and on the advice of a colleague on my EdD, I joined Twitter. I saw an article being shared online that Caroline Spalding had written about teachers and tattoos, where she shared her opinion that teachers should hide them for work. I have almost a full bodysuit of tattoos, so not only would hiding them be impossible, I also fundamentally disagree that teachers should have to. I contacted Caroline to respectfully share my opinion and she was gracious enough to write a follow-up piece where she included my soundbite, which was then published in TES. I caught the bug! As I began to build followers on Twitter, I submitted another article on TES and was thrilled to see that this time it was accepted and was even given the cover story in their magazine.

I joined Twitter at a time when education publishing was becoming a really booming business and writing a book was no longer just the preserve of academics, teachers were being given a voice and it was all very exciting. I could see lots of teachers around me publishing books – many of whom had been teaching for less time than me, hadn't had my experiences of working in challenging, special measures schools and were not professional writers . . . so I thought, why shouldn't I give it a go? But the problem was that I didn't really know where to start.

Q2. How were you able to secure a publisher?

I had my idea for two books initially: Humans in the classroom, which is a compendium of incredible teacher's stories from around the world, and Preserving positivity, which is a book for experienced teachers about overcoming the challenges that teaching brings.

Two inspirational friends and colleagues helped me with securing publishing deals. Debbie Kidd lives close by and I taught her son and we also taught at the same school, so we had lots of mutual acquaintances and lots in common. Debbie has had quite a few books published and works around the world as a consultant; she pretty much had my dream life, so I met her for a gin at a local pub and picked her brains. I told her about my book idea for Humans in the classroom and she said she knew the perfect publisher. Within a couple of days I had been introduced to Caroline at McNidder and Grace and had filled in an author questionnaire. I couldn't believe it when the book was accepted and I was sent a contract setting out the terms. Again, a real pinch myself moment. I owe Debbie a lot, she also *introduced me to Ian Gilbert who runs Independent Thinking Limited and joining their books as an associate absolutely changed my life.*

The second book, Preserving positivity, *was a harder sell, and I didn't have the first idea about who to approach with it. I had recently read a fantastic book by Jennifer Webb and after meeting her at a conference, I sent her a Twitter message and asked her whether she could offer some guidance. She was incredibly generous and sent me the email address of John Catt, while also giving me some tips about what they might ask for. Again, I filled in an author questionnaire and was flabbergasted when my book was accepted.*

I have never forgotten the kindness of these two colleagues and my next book, Mentoring in schools, *was dedicated to them, alongside other fabulous mentors I have had in my own career. By this time, I felt like an old hat at publishing and knew what to expect when pitching my next three books. But each publisher has different processes, so the journey isn't always identical to this.*

Q3. What was your writing schedule and how did you manage to write about education in addition to your other professional responsibilities and family life?

With my first book, I left it ridiculously close to the deadline to start writing it. This was due to trying to juggle a small baby, a teenager, a PhD and full-time teaching. I had also taken on a PR job at a vintage glasses company, so it all kept me busy!

The deadline was in May during school closures due to the pandemic and I managed to bash the whole 60,000 words out in just six weeks. The second and third books took about six months each, but I was more sensible with them and wrote a little bit every day during my PPA at school or at 15:30 when the students left. Inevitably when you are balancing a lot, it does involve some evening and weekend work too.

The two books I am currently working on now have taken what seems like an age as now I have left teaching, I am juggling even more. I am now a principal lecturer overseeing mentoring training and support with over a thousand mentors, as well as strategically leading education input at IRIS Connect, speaking all over the world as a consultant and attempting to finish my Doctoral dissertation! I sometimes take a break of a few weeks and it takes me ages to get back into it. My advice would be to try and dedicate between one and two hours to it a day and a bit longer at weekends.

Q4. What are the main challenges in terms of writing about education?

I think the challenges are that there are no certainties, only best bets! Much educational research can be quite abstract, which is fine by the way. But I want classroom teachers to read my books and get something tangible out of it. Therefore, it can be quite a task to translate complex academic papers into digestible forms and consider the implications for classroom practice.

I am also a secondary specialist, and schools are much more than secondaries. Therefore, I have needed to call on the expertise of colleagues in primary, Early Years Foundation Stage (EYFS) and FE lots to be able to write with any kind of authority on these topics.

Teachers can also be some of the loudest critics. There is a real divide in education at the moment, which comes from silly tribalistic labels, such as progressive ('prog') and traditionalists ('trad'). In reality, most teachers are somewhere in the middle, but the most extreme voices are often the loudest, so putting yourself out there as a writer leaves you open to nasty subtweets and attacks on social media. Sometimes, I am not sure I always have the stomach for it. Lots of professional jealousy also exists and I have seen tweets about 'bloggers', 'authors' and 'edu-celebs' being described as know-alls, etc. My response would be that most people like me who write books aren't professing to have all the answers, or that their way is the only way. They are just a teacher, having the bravery to put themselves out there and share something which has worked for them.

Q5. Once your books have been published, how have you promoted them and can you offer any advice about self-promotion?

I find this the most difficult part! Of course, you can constantly tweet about it but this soon annoys people and puts them off actually reading your work. Some of the things that have worked for me have included:

● Holding a launch event with different speakers

● Doing radio and TV interviews

● Writing related articles for newspapers and magazines (not just education focused)

● Speaking about things in your book at schools and events.

The education market is flooded with books and some publishers are churning them out at a rate of knots. It depends on who your publisher is, but some publishers do also help massively with publicity and will arrange and send you lots of opportunities alongside your own efforts.

Q6. Why do you enjoy writing about education and what are the rewards and benefits?

It is fair to say that my third book, Mentoring in schools, has completely changed my life and given my career a rocket boost. Both my employers for my two jobs read the book and approached me to apply for my current positions after reading it. In addition, it has led to me to becoming one of England's most well-known experts on mentoring novice teachers, which has taken me the length and breadth of the country delivering workshops and keynotes and will enable me to speak in Brussels, Seville and Rome in the next six months alone.

I sometimes struggle with the fact that I am no longer at the chalk face. The impact I am making now is much wider but I still do miss the interaction with the students. My career is incredibly exciting though and I would never have got these opportunities without my books.

Q7. What advice would you offer to someone wanting to follow a similar career path to you?

Get involved in teacher development wherever you can. That might look like delivering CPD in your own school or trust and applying to facilitate government mandated qualifications like the Early Career Framework (ECF) and NPQs at your local teaching school hub. You could also contact your local ITTE (Information Technology in Teacher Education) provider and offer to run some sessions as they are always looking to work with subject/phase specialists.

In terms of speaking, get yourself out there and apply to speak at some teach meets or conferences. The first time I did it a few years ago, I felt physically sick but it does get easier and it is a great way of getting yourself known and spreading your ideas.

The writing is connected to all of this, as when you fill in an author questionnaire they will ask you if you speak at conferences and what other writing you have done, such as blogging or for magazines. They want to see whether there will be a market for your book and whether you can help them publicise it and sell copies.

In terms of pitching your book, do your research. Are there other books which are similar? If there are, how is your work different? What is its USP (unique selling position)? Be clear about who the book's core market is and what people who buy it will get from it.

I would also say, join Twitter. It is a fantastic online community and yes, it can sometimes be a bit of a bin fire, but the more you curate your timeline the better it will be. The mute button is your friend! So many of the opportunities I have got have been from connections there, including the chance to be part of this excellent book!

Q8. What are your future goals, aspirations and ambitions?

I have so many. I have another couple of ideas for books which I am yet to pitch. I also want to become a university professor and get an OBE (Order of the British Empire)! I would love to take my Grandma to the palace. I will be 40 in 2023 and

I am pretty happy with my achievements so far but am always incapable of sitting still . . . lots to still strive for.

Q9. Why do you think is it important and necessary that more women write about education?

I think for too long the loudest voices in education have been older white men. I go to a lot of conferences, and you can almost play bingo with some of the names who you know will be there speaking. That isn't to say that these men haven't got great things to say. David Didau for instance is somebody who has been on the conference circuit and writing books since I was a trainee sixteen years ago and I learn something every time I read or listen to his work. But women and teachers and leaders from minority ethnic backgrounds also deserve to have their voice heard.

I love seeing other women succeed and like to surround myself with women who light one another's candles, not extinguish them. Education is all the better for their presence. Education giants like Mary Myatt and Christine Counsell have really shaped the way that I think about education and teaching and I hope to be part of continuing their legacy.

Thank you to Haili Hughes for contributing to this book, sharing her wonderful experiences and honest advice as a best-selling author in education.

The writing process

Like Haili Hughes and many other female authors in education, I wrote books whilst teaching full time. This was tough and certainly did involve hours in the evenings and weekends but it is certainly possible. I was able to achieve this due to a supportive team of colleagues at the schools I worked at and a publisher that was flexible, accommodating and understood teaching was my priority. Classroom teachers have an authentic voice and are able to share real life classroom examples that others will relate to or learn from. It is important to be mindful of workload and commitments throughout the writing process.

Writing any extended piece requires increased screen time. Healthline.com have warned that too much screen time can result in digital eye strain, fatigue, head and neck pain and other threats. It is important to take regular breaks. If you are in a flow of creativity, it can help to write ideas and notes on paper that can be typed up later.

There are no set rules about writing a book, different authors will have different approaches. Some writers are flexible and write whenever they have the time and motivation. Other writers are more disciplined and will create a strict schedule and routine to stick to. Regardless of the approach, writing a book requires self-determination, motivation and resilience. There can be days where writing flows easily and other days when writer's block can hit hard.

Variables will influence how and when a book is written. Some publishers set specific deadlines that authors are contracted and obliged to meet, whereas others are more flexible with their deadline and will happily increase the deadline if required. Other commitments need to be taken into consideration, ranging from other work responsibilities to personal circumstances. I would always advise a writer to allow themselves more time than they need because life happens and an unexpected disruption can interrupt a writing schedule.

I was quite naive to believe being pregnant wouldn't impact my ability to write or interfere with my planning. Sickness and headaches occurred on days that I had kept free to write and therefore I was unable to. I found I wasn't able to write at the pace I had previously done with my other books, I was experiencing fatigue and this had an impact on my productivity. I told my publisher about my pregnancy and they were very supportive. I was aware if I needed an extension with my deadline to support my workload and pregnancy, it was possible.

Not all writers approach their books in a chronological order. It is important to have an outline of the book and the chapters included but this should be completed before the writing process takes place. There may be some chapters that are easier or more enjoyable to write than others. It is important to ensure consistency throughout the book and aim to have a similar word count for each chapter. If other people are contributing to your book, like the interviews and case studies in this book, that needs to be factored into the overall word count for each chapter too.

It can be a great idea to include others in your book, as there may be gaps in your knowledge, experience and expertise that someone else can share. The inclusion of other individuals in your book can be a celebration and showcase of their hard work, story or talent. It is important to give contributors plenty of time and as much clear guidance and structure as possible to ensure the contributions flow with the overall tone, themes and content of your book.

Promoting your book

Once a book has been through a rigorous editing process and is published, this may feel like the end of a journey but it is the beginning of launching and promoting the book to attract readers. A publisher should contribute to the marketing of a new book but this alone is not enough. The author will need to promote the book as widely as possible.

There are various ways to promote books, including the following:

- Share the book and positive reviews widely across different social media platforms (as many as possible)

- Take part in podcast/radio interviews to discuss the contents of the book

- Ask individuals to provide reviews and share reviews with their networks and following

- Attend events to talk about the content of the book and encourage audience members to purchase the book

- Host online competitions. I have done this with several of my books through Twitter. I ran a competition which involved people retweeting a post about my book and one winner would be selected at random (I use https://retweetpicker.com/). Through others retweeting a post about a book, this advertises the book to other social media users.

- Deliver a launch event to celebrate the release of the book and generate discussion about the book.

Women can struggle with the aspect of self-promotion, but it is an important element of being a successful writer and published author. Published content was written with the intention of providing interest, support or advice to readers. There are a lot of articles, blogs and books available in the field of education so self-promotion is necessary to ensure your writing stands out and is read.

Writing can offer many benefits such as the ability to reflect, share and earn an additional income. Writing can vary from recording personal thoughts, to a formal qualification, contributing to magazines or authoring a book. Education is a field dominated by women, therefore it is vital women are writing about education.

6 Public speaking

Speaking or presenting to an audience is part of the day-to-day job for any classroom teacher or school leader. Considering how often educators are expected to speak publicly, it is surprising there isn't more discussion, training and advice about how to do so with confidence and do so effectively.

Teachers stand up in front of their students every day, leading and delivering lessons. A Head of Year will regularly host an assembly for the year group they lead. Senior leaders are expected to present to large audiences of students, parents and teachers. If any teacher aspires to school leadership then it is highly likely, or inevitable, this will entail public speaking. It is a necessary part of the job description and tends to be unavoidable.

There are also plentiful opportunities for those in education to speak publicly outside of their school environment. The rise of TeachMeet events (informal conferences open to all to share, reflect and network) and conferences across the UK and beyond has led to increased opportunities for people across the profession to speak up and present to their peers. There is a responsibility for event organisers to ensure a range of diverse speakers are invited and are included. However, some events are open to all, and the organisers do not invite people to speak and rely solely on volunteers.

Women must be present at events, as attendees and speakers. Women should be delivering keynote presentations, leading workshops, and invited to be part of panel discussions. WomenEd have coined the term 'manel' referring to a male only panel, and they are rightly calling out events and panel discussions that exclude women from the conversation.

Deborah Shames, co-founder of Eloqui (a company focused on communication and presentations, based in the US) and author of the best-selling book *Own the room* (2009) has stated; *'While women have advanced in many arenas, women will never achieve their potential if they avoid public speaking'*. Women are certainly present at conferences and events but we need to keep ensuring this and encouraging more women in education to stand on the platform so they can be seen and heard.

DOI: 10.4324/9781003380528-7

Why can women be reluctant public speakers?

In the paper, *'Do women shy away from public speaking? A field experiment'* (February 2020), the authors conducted an experiment with 500 undergraduate students who could gain two extra points to their final exam grade by orally presenting solutions to a specific problem set. The findings showed that women were willing to present in a face-to-face situation but were *'considerably less likely to give a public presentation'*. There can be a range of factors that prevent women from putting themselves forward to speak in front of their peers and to an audience. It is often assumed that women are reluctant to speak publicly for the following reasons.

- A lack of confidence or shyness related to presenting in front of others

- Anxiety linked to speaking in public

- Imposter syndrome

- Family or personal commitments that make it difficult to attend events outside of working hours

- Women facing scrutiny based on their clothing, appearance and presentation style

- Being uncomfortable with an act of self-promotion.

These certainly can be relevant reasons for some women, but not always. A *Forbes* article published in 2018 entitled, *'Why women say no to public speaking'*, suggested there are alternative reasons as to why women turn down opportunities related to public speaking. *Forbes* noted that *'women are more likely to work part time than men'*, meaning it is not possible to attend events or they may not be considered or asked to present as a part-time employee in favour of someone working full time. Working part time can be linked with another reason suggested by *Forbes*, *'Women have more additional responsibilities outside of work than men'*. This would then suggest that women need to have a strong support network inside and outside of work so they are able to take advantage of such opportunities.

Forbes also added that women can become overbooked with engagements. This can certainly be true of high-profile women in education that simply cannot attend every public speaking opportunity. The simple solution to this is to promote more women across the profession so there isn't simply one woman to go to for leadership, curriculum, safeguarding or teaching and learning but instead a range of female expertise is available.

The *Forbes* article offered useful advice to event managers and organisers to encourage more women to present, and it involved giving female speakers as much advance notice as possible, being flexible with timings and scheduling to accommodate female speakers and being upfront about fees and payment.

It is vital that organisations and companies are transparent about payments to ensure there is not an unfair gender pay gap. The fee for speaking at conferences can vary considerably, from no fee to payment involving thousands of pounds. Conferences should pay all speakers the same rate, but this does not always happen. Individuals will have their own rates and often do not share these figures publicly but that can result in a large disparity across speakers presenting at the same event. It is often considered unprofessional to discuss payments, and this is regarded as an area of privacy but this creates a barrier to transparency about pay and closing the gender pay gap.

Beyond conferences there are also opportunities within the media, as media outlets tend to reach out to speak to experts in education to discuss the latest news story or gain a unique insight from someone in the sector. There are educators that have delivered TED or TEDx Talks that have gained thousands (or even millions) of views online. Public speaking has evolved from a traditional model of speaking to an audience in front of you to the ability to reach audiences online across continents and time zones, live or recorded.

Spotlight: Rita Pierson

Rita Pierson was an educator in America for over forty years, beginning her teaching career in 1972. Pierson taught elementary school, junior high and special education with roles including a counsellor, testing coordinator and assistant principal. Later in her career Pierson focused on leading professional development for teachers through hosting workshops and seminars for thousands of teachers.

Pierson has become known globally due to her famous TED Talk delivered in 2013, 'Every kid needs a champion'. The TED Talk has received over 5.8 million views and over 74K likes (at the time of writing). The main message of the TED Talk is that every child needs a teacher or adult to be their champion. If you haven't viewed this TED Talk, I recommend doing so. If you have viewed it before, I would suggest revisiting it, watching with a focus on her brilliant public speaking skills.

As a public speaker Pierson is able to connect with an audience through story-telling and her down-to-earth manner. She was able to make the audience laugh, think and reflect. Pierson started with a strong opener, an insight into her personal life sharing that her grandparents and parents were classroom teachers and she naturally followed in their footsteps. Pierson doesn't use any slides in her presentation but it is under eight minutes, and TED Talk presenters are required to thoroughly rehearse and prepare their talk.

Pierson uses quotes throughout her talk to support the points she makes and she discusses important issues such as poverty, low school attendance and negative peer influences. There has been some critique of the content of her presentation as Pierson famously stated, 'Kids don't learn from people they don't like', and this has been contested by educators that students can learn from teachers that they may not like on a personal level. Despite that, most if not all will agree with the core message of her talk about the importance and value of relationships. Pierson directly addresses the audience stating, 'Everyone in this room has been affected by a teacher or adult'. Audience members can be seen nodding along in agreement, and no doubt this will resonate with online viewers too.

Pierson spoke clearly, raising her voice at different points for emphasis and making use of facial expressions and hand gestures. Throughout her talk Pierson shared personal stories from her experiences as a classroom teacher and was able to make the audience laugh and hold on to their attention and focus throughout.

Rita Pierson died in 2013, yet her TED Talk continues to inspire teachers around the world.

Public speaking can fill people with dread, excitement or a range of other emotions somewhere in between. It can often feel that some people are simply natural public speakers and others aren't. Whilst it is clearly true that some people are more comfortable on a stage and in front of an audience more than others, it is a skill that can be developed.

I have been very fortunate to speak at events around the world ranging from across the UK, Middle East, Hong Kong, Thailand, Africa, New Zealand and more. They have involved a combination of in-person and online presentations. There are pros and cons to speaking online or in person.

The benefits and pros of speaking in person include:

- An opportunity to engage directly with an audience

- The chance to network and meet others

- Opportunity to travel to a different school or location

- An overall memorable experience.

The benefits and pros of speaking online include:

- Flexibility to work from home/school without the need for travel (this is cheaper and more environmentally friendly and won't require as much time and energy)

- The potential to reach a wider audience with an online platform

- A pre-recorded session allows the presenter to edit/amend a presentation before sharing with others

- It can be less nerve wracking to present online and not be confronted with a visible audience in front of you.

Presenting online or in person requires many of the same key skills, but there is a difference and people do have their preferences. Prior to Covid-19 I was invited to speak at many conferences in the UK, but at the time I was based in Abu Dhabi and it was simply too far and too costly to attend. During the pandemic and the 'Zoom Boom', I was able to view presentations and present directly from my home in Abu Dhabi. Zoom fatigue meant that many people, myself included, were keen to embrace the return to face-to-face events in order to interact with an audience and take advantage of networking opportunities.

During my pregnancy my preference has been to present online. This avoids travel (which has increased in cost with fuel prices and public transport has become challenging with the strikes in 2022/23) and can save a huge amount of time (depending on location).

If delivering an in-person session, I may need to travel by car for example three hours there and back, so although the session was 60–90 minutes, most of my day would be taken up by travel. If the keynote presentation is international that further increases costs and travel. I can cope much easier with online presentations during a time in my life when I am experiencing exhaustion and need to take great care with my health and wellbeing. However, prior to my pregnancy I would seize any opportunity to present internationally and combine that opportunity with my passion for travel and exploration.

If you are a public speaker and wish to improve or are considering speaking publicly, in front of colleagues or at an external event, there are different aspects to be aware of to help boost confidence and increase enjoyment when speaking publicly.

Presentation design

Most teachers will use a presentation tool during their lessons, from PowerPoint to Google Slides, Canva or a similar alternative. The slides in a presentation are not the presentation, the presenter is. The slides are there to assist both the presenter and the audience. It is simply a tool and aid and should only be viewed that way. Despite the fact the slides are secondary to the presenter, it is worth investing time and effort into presentation design.

I can recall presenting at an event and due to technical difficulties, I was unable to access my PowerPoint presentation. For twenty minutes I froze and apologised to the audience, waiting for the technical team to fix the problem. I lacked the confidence to talk without my slides or use that opportunity to interact with the audience. On reflection this was not the best way to handle that situation. I am now confident as a presenter and with my content, to talk without slides if I needed to (although it can be useful to have a backup presentation online or on a USB device).

Presentation slides should act as a prompt and guidance for the speaker, a reminder what to discuss and in which order. The slides can help the audience to visualise, understand or engage more with the content being discussed. Design principles are fundamental and just as they can be applied to the classroom to support teaching and learning, they can and should be considered with public speaking.

Cognitive load theory, based on the work of Professor John Sweller, has been described by Dylan Wiliam as '*the single most important thing for teachers to know*'.[1] This was in reference to teaching and learning in the classroom, but knowledge of cognitive load theory can also support speakers when designing and using presentation slides. Cognitive load theory is based on the limitations of working memory, although working memory capacity can vary, it is widely accepted that everyone has limitations in terms of how much information they can hold in working memory and for how long.

As working memory can only process so much information at one given time, it can become easily overloaded. Therefore presentation slides that contain too much text or irrelevant images that are on display at the same time the presenter is speaking is likely to result in cognitive overload. Audience members can become distracted or overwhelmed by the content. It would be advisable to use bold headings and clear images supported by a verbal explanation. Text can be included in a presentation, but this should be kept to a minimum and used to focus on key points, statistics or information that the presenter can elaborate and discuss further.

Dual coding is another evidence informed teaching and learning strategy that can be applied to presentation design and delivery. This involves presenting information in two formats – images and text, or images and a verbal explanation – to emphasise points clearly and make the content more memorable.

It is important to select images that are clear, relevant and add to your presentation, not distract. Another essential point is to ensure that any images used are available royalty free, to avoid any copyright problems. There are a vast number of images online that are protected, and sharing them in a public domain can lead to difficulties and a possible financial penalty. There are websites that offer a wide choice of high-quality stock images that can be used freely. These websites include:

- Pixabay.com
- Canva.com
- Pexels.com
- Unsplash.com
- Flickr.com

In terms of presentation design simplicity is key. Ensure the font is clear for all to read (there may be audience members with impaired vision). Avoid complicated transitions, animations and anything that is not relevant. I would recommend every presenter purchase their own electronic presentation clicker (to transition smoothly between slides and allow freedom to move away from the computer mouse) as not all venues will provide this, and spare batteries are also useful! If a presenter is confident with their subject knowledge and has a genuine interest and enthusiasm, this will shine through, and the presentation is simply a tool to support and enhance.

Presentation timings

Timing a presentation accurately can be challenging and there can be variables that interfere with the timings of the day or your session. I have invested hours rehearsing a presentation to ensure I wouldn't finish with plenty of time left or finish without sharing all of the content of my presentation. Despite my best efforts, timings don't always go to plan for a range of reasons. Here are some examples, all based on my own experiences, which had an impact on the timings of my presentation.

- Due to traffic, strikes or other external factors the audience were late to an event and the hosts decided to delay the timings but still expected me as the speaker to finish at the original time, reducing a presentation from 60 minutes to 45 minutes.

- The host welcomed the audience and introduced me as a speaker and this took five minutes, that was five minutes of my presentation time and five minutes that I was expected to cut back.

- The person presenting before did not finish on time and their lateness then had an impact on how long I had to present (something to consider and be aware of if someone is speaking after you).

- Last minute changes to the schedule of the day have meant I have had to be flexible and adapt accordingly with very little notice.

Speaker requirements

If you are an external speaker, the host may ask if you have any requirements. It is easy to resort to saying no, to avoid appearing like a diva, but there are reasonable requests that can be made to support your overall experience. A host may not ask if there is anything you require, and this can make it difficult to ask but it can help to have the following:

- A designated parking space at the venue. This can save a lot of time and potentially avoid a stressful arrival. If you are arriving by taxi or public transport then inform the host and ask for any advice or assistance to ensure you arrive at the location without stress or struggle.

- Water available for before, during and after your presentation to stay hydrated and support your voice. I have found this to be essential!

- Ensure the host can cope with any technical demands, for example, if you need Wi-Fi or to show a video or have audio during your presentation, it is worth checking in advance that it is possible and if so ask them to prepare for that.

I have hearing loss in my left ear and wear a hearing aid, and one specific requirement I have had to ask for in the past is a microphone for audience members during a live question and answer discussion, as I can often struggle to hear from a distance. There may be other requests you have and some things you may bring yourself, for example, water and your laptop. It is not demanding to make requests that are reasonable and that will support your delivery and performance on the day.

Presenting

It can be difficult to present when nerves have taken over. I have witnessed this many times with the speaker appearing to panic, their voice shaking and a red face or sweat becoming visible. This can make audience members uncomfortable, and although nerves are common it is important to try to relax on stage. Preparing and planning can help reduce nerves and confidence can grow and develop.

The pace of a presentation is important. Too slow and the audience may become restless, and too fast can lead to content being lost or not fully understood by audience members. In addition to pace is volume. A microphone can help but is not always available, hence the importance of water and looking after the greatest tool a presenter can have, their voice. Ensure pronunciation is clear, if there are long or complicated words, aim to replace them if possible with words that won't make you stumble or hesitate.

Every presenter has something worth sharing. Try as much as possible to enjoy the experience and view it as an opportunity to learn and develop.

Feedback

Any teacher knows and understands the importance of feedback to improve and make progress. The same can be applied with public speaking. However, be careful about when and how you seek feedback. Feedback can be personal, and it can also be very subjective. I can recall receiving feedback from a particular session where I was praised for including a wide range of examples during the session, but another member of that audience gave feedback that said I should aim to include more examples. This was conflicting feedback and not very helpful. I reflected on this feedback, dwelling more so on the negative than positive, and realised more examples would mean less time to discuss the examples, rushing through content to add more content and was there a possibility of too many examples? This was a classic case of you can't please everyone!

Ask someone you know and trust for some kind, specific and helpful feedback. Ask about content, delivery, pace and presence. Do not ask anyone to grade your presentation as 'outstanding' or 'requires improvement' because those labels don't help. One audience member may describe the presentation as wonderful and another satisfactory, based on a range of reasons and opinions.

If possible, it can be a useful activity to watch yourself present, this is much easier with a virtual presentation that is recorded. It is important not to be too critical but also try to find the areas for development.

Interview: Jaz Ampaw-Farr

Bio: As CEO of London-based Human First Ltd, Jaz Ampaw-Farr helps leaders who want to influence, inspire and motivate their teams with greater engagement in order to grow their businesses and leave a lifelong legacy. Jaz combines lessons learned from a challenging and often brutal childhood with those from her rise to teacher, coach, TV presenter, TEDx speaker, stand-up comedian and reality TV star (former candidate on *The Apprentice*). Her authentic honesty and humour consistently empower people to think differently about leading themselves and others.

Jaz delivers bespoke and interactive stand out keynotes around the following themes: Human-First Leadership, Future-proofed Wellbeing, Belonging and Diversity and Mental Resilience. To find out more about Jaz, you can visit her website http://www.jazampawfarr.com/.

Q1. Jaz you are very well known in education, and beyond, as an inspirational and motivational public speaker. Can you tell us about how you got to this point?

I was homeless while I was at university, I didn't have anywhere to live. I slept on the streets at Christmas because students were kicked out of university accommodation for the holidays. The first two years at university I was literally homeless. I was sofa surfing in the holidays, and I knew if I could just get a degree my life would be different. But it just felt impossible. Totally impossible and so it was hell.

Then when I started teaching that was also very difficult. I did my first job in Clacton-on-Sea and the racism on its own was hideous. It was hard and I didn't get any support from the school. But then I started teaching and it was fantastic. Teaching was my first love, my absolute first love. I was doing a lot of literacy because reading, writing and spelling are tickets out of poverty. I was always interested in literacy and phonics. There was still a phonics argument but I was using

Jolly Phonics and my kids were reading and writing in reception class. Another school asked me how I did it, so I started sharing ideas and talking to parents.

I then went to Chris Jolly and his publisher and said, 'You need to give me some free resources, I'm doing advertising for you!'. He said, 'Do you want to come into a talk?' I thought, are you cracking on to me?! So I went with him on the Friday to talk to Headteachers. He shared all this data and stats and I just talked about my kids and what they were doing and showed some of the kids' work. I did that talk for him and that's how I got into literacy and started speaking at events.

I worked with the government, I advised governments internationally and I was on the first committee for assessing phonics schemes for the DfE match funding. I advised international governments on Education Policy and it got to the point where I realised I wasn't being honest. People would say, 'Oh, you came to our authorities twenty years ago, and you talked about phonics and now we're all doing this'. I thought great, but I just wasn't being honest about why education, and literacy in particular, was so important to me. I couldn't dream of telling anyone, I was so scared.

I was hiding my X Factor backstory, because what would happen if the staff or parents found out that I was an abused child, because now am I safe in front of other people's kids? I couldn't cope with that. I had to just push everything back so that I'd appear acceptable. I've crafted this professional persona and I never wanted to lose it.

Later I went on to coaching with teachers and I was doing lots of training on growth mindset. I realised that a lot of the teachers I was speaking to, didn't have a growth mindset and neither did the school leaders. They had an attitude focused on getting the kids to try harder, but they weren't prepared to do it themselves. You can tell your kid to swim without being able to swim, you just watch a video and put those blue things on your shoes. You don't get in the pool. But if you want to teach, if you want to embed ambitious resilience, you better get wet. I thought this is not good enough.

I was invited to do a talk about literacy at a TeachMeet event in London and I thought, I wonder what would happen if I just told the truth? I swapped my slides, and I gave a little bit of my story. I trended for the second time in history (the first time being when I was fired from The Apprentice during week one, which was horrible trending!). The second time was because it just resonated, the very thing that I was afraid people would find out about me that I didn't have it all together was the very thing that gave people agency. After I did that, that's when I got the TEDx Talk and a book deal and international speaking gigs and it's from showing up as myself.

I spoke about it at WomenEd events a lot as well. It was difficult because I've got the biggest secret and I felt I've got to keep it. Education is one area of my life that has cost me everything. I've worked so hard to be a teacher I couldn't mess it up. I used to pretend I had a brother called Tarquin and I used to lie about my family.

I said my parents were dead and I went to boarding school but I finally decided to tell the truth about myself and that was massive. It totally paid off.

I set up my own business. I set up a consultancy for education, and I just played by my rules, because it's set up for you to lose, when you have maternity leave and go back to education. I decided I'll change the rules and then I'll play again and I can win. I set up my education consultancy and went full time delivering phonics training and actually made more money than teaching. I'm not interested in being a school leader. I always want, even now, to be with the kids in a classroom. I want to be in a reception class, smashing it, teaching kids how to read, write and spell. That's it.

Q2. You are clearly very confident as a public speaker, where does your confidence come from and do you have any advice for someone lacking confidence?

It's not confidence, it's being comfortable. I'm comfortable with failure and this is massive. Imagine living like you've got nothing to fear, nothing to lose and nothing to prove. That's how I live.

I was someone who let fear drive my bus, I was a passenger in my own life terrified on the backseat, crying with my head down. That's how I lived my life and I compared myself to everyone else all the time. I'd look at what other teachers were doing and look at myself, my backstage, their front stage on Twitter and think I'm a terrible person or I'm not good enough. I was constantly afraid.

I think confidence is tied to resilience, and it's tied to failing and I'm a failure ninja! I'm a mistake artist. I felt so much and when I was about to speak I used to feel sick. I would panic and say, 'Oh my god, what if I fall over? What if I fall down the steps? What if I forget my points? What if my slides don't work? What if no one laughs? What if everyone laughs at me?' All of those things I realise are all about me. They're all about self-preservation. They're all about me looking stupid. So instead of having the lever on what if I do something to look stupid? Why am I doing this? I turn the lever from me onto the audience.

I stopped thinking about me and I started thinking about people who've left emails, put their kids in childcare, have got other things on their mind, but have come today in the hope that I might say one thing that will help them get out of where they've been trapped for years and move forward. Then I'm not worried because I'm not thinking about myself. I'm thinking about why I am here and I am showing up as my full self. That is not confidence. It's comfortable.

It's also a deep desire for change. I want to change more than I want to be right. I want to be right a lot but I want change more and that requires inconveniencing myself. Everyone wants things to be better in education, but nobody wants change. You can't have one without the other so pick a side. For me, change is inconvenient so I will inconvenience myself. It's not confidence. Everything that could go wrong for me has gone wrong. I've faced bigger and scarier things than falling upstage or my slides not working. I can do my keynote without slides because I share my story and I can't forget that.

I've been the only brown person in the room and the only woman at the confer-ence. I can't tell you how many white males have given me their coat at the door while I'm welcoming him into the conference. I take the coat on stage with me and ask for the highest bidder starting at a pound! Some people use slides as a script and look around while reading it but I've just got pictures on mine and I just engage people in what I'm doing.

It's about showing up as human first and professional second. Second, that's the difference. My company is actually called Human First, because the strapline is about meeting people where they are, and if you're nervous, it's because you're worried about you and not them. If you don't care enough about the audience and to be invested, then don't speak. The world is waiting for you and your unique message so don't be selfish by keeping it to yourself.

I still worry and obsess over things. I've got resources and things that I can do or use but my default setting is worry. I choose not to live like that, because I've tried being fed up and suicidal and distressed and depressed. It sucks. So I do the work required to not have that be driving my story.

Q3. Do you think you have grown, developed and progressed as a public speaker? If so, how?

I tell people to watch my TEDx Talk but that was four years ago, and I am a master, I am phenomenal at this. I have mastered the art of connecting with an audience, meeting them where they are taking them from laughter to tears and back to laugh-ter in two sentences. I make them laugh, cry and leave on a high at the end and that is standard for me. I'm trying to get sponsorship with Kleenex because I do make people cry a lot!

People tell me 'you're one of the best speakers I've seen' and virtual as well. Well, I can be speaking to 7,000 people at Leeds arena and or speaking to 7,000 people in my pandemic proof studio, wherever I am I can reach you into your heart. I feel like repetition makes you better and this week is my 2,900th keynote presentation. I'm not going to do any more after 3,000. I'm not going to tell my story after 3,000 because it's all out there and my book will be out.

After every talk, people disclose their own abuse or whatever's happened and sometimes they say they want to do what I'm doing. I tell people they are looking at forty years of work. It's not like I sat on the sofa, my fingers crossed, hoping everything would turn out. Do you first, you cannot start talking about issues that have not been processed. It's really dangerous. All this kind of rehearsed, practice, confidence, whatever people want to call it, is the result of doing the work and doing the work makes you excellent. I am excellent. I would say I am one of, if not the best, speakers in education and outside of education I'm pretty much up there.

Outside of education I charge £18,000 pounds for a keynote for an hour. In education I discount it massively, because that's what it is. I give money back to put into my academy and on my website there's loads of free stuff available to help others.

Q4. Clearly you enjoy public speaking and some wonder how you can enjoy it. It can be terrifying, daunting and uncomfortable. What do you enjoy about it?

I don't like the fame aspect of it. I like to go somewhere and no one knows who I am. One guy spilt his coffee down me once and like a woman I said sorry! He said, oh, yeah, and gave me a tissue and sort of went off. Then I did the keynote and he came and found me afterwards and said, 'Oh my god, I didn't know it was you. I'm so sorry'. I was a human before and I'm a human now. So I really struggle with that, and someone actually asked if they could touch me and I said you can have a hug, but nothing's going to wear off! I don't mind doing selfies because I know how I feel when someone who is genuinely famous agrees to do a selfie with me. That's exciting but I just find it hard.

What I'm trying to do is make people feel that anything is possible. But when they come to me and say you're inspirational, I say great, what have I inspired you to do? And they don't know. I haven't inspired them. I've just piqued their interest. So what they're thinking is: you're great, but there's no way I could do it, which means I've failed, because my whole point is listening to me and then going, this is what I'm going to change. There's celebrity and Twitter celebrity status. I'm not good at that and I don't like that. But I enjoy speaking and I'm a connector. I connect people to ideas.

I want my own Netflix show. That's what I'm doing next. People ask what are you going to do next? I reply, I'm having a Netflix show and nobody has gone, 'That's, that's weird'. Everyone says that sounds about right.

Q5. How can we encourage more women to enter the field and arena of public speaking?

If you're at the stage where you're doing something because you want to help other people to thrive, then share your story. How other people thrive is by knowing that someone's gone before them and you, no matter where you think you are in your journey, are further ahead than other people who cannot even believe that the stage you're at exists. So for me, it's about being the woman you were designed to be, not the woman the world tells you, you have to be.

I feel like I have a responsibility and it's an invitation, but also a duty to hold the door open for people who are behind me. This all started with the TEDx Talk because I literally knew that I knew how to survive and thrive and drive change, and I wasn't talking about it. I was literally stealing that opportunity from other people. And the world is waiting for the unique thoughts and gifts that only you have. So by not sharing it, I mean, that's even if you don't believe in God, you get a given account at the end of your life and you're going to sit there and go, Yeah, I didn't say anything. Because, you know, well, it's not, I don't want to, I don't want to share what I know. Because someone else might benefit. You are in education therefore your whole life itself is to benefit others.

People often say I could talk in front of the kids, but not adults. First of all the wrong way round, because the kids have no filters and they will tell you what they think and adults will wind their neck in. So you should really do it the other way. Secondly, that's like saying that the kids aren't as important as your peers. The kids are important. You're important and your peers are important.

The worst thing that can happen is that everything goes right the first time and you miss out on an opportunity to learn, reframe and pivot and embed resilience. That's the worst thing that can happen. Not that you fail. Let's say you should be aiming for epic failure, because that's why I'm so good. I've failed so much. You either win or learn. You can only get to success by failure. There is no other route.

Thank you to Jaz for sharing her story, including her highs and lows, with excellent advice for women in education.

Top tips for public speaking

Don't wait for an opportunity to speak publicly, find it and seize it. This could be volunteering at your school to deliver an assembly, lead a CPD session or signing up to speak at an event.

Know your stuff! Invest time and effort creating a presentation that is interesting, informative and allows you to share your passion, knowledge and expertise with an audience.

Repeat that presentation at different events and to different audiences as much as you can. This will allow you to tweak and refine, instead of constantly creating new content from scratch. Repeating presentations allows the presenter to know which slide comes next without looking at the screen and visibly grow in confidence and feel more comfortable with their content.

If you are trying to build a profile and become recognised as a public speaker, be prepared to be patient. Event organisers do tend to ask individuals to speak that have gained a reputation and established themselves as a public speaker or ask individuals that are recommended by others. To get to that point will take a lot of time (it could take months or even years) and effort, and it could be costly initially. Not every public speaking opportunity will be paid or will be local, and it might have to happen outside of normal working hours, for example, an evening or weekend. Through resilience and practise it is possible to become a credible and authentic public speaker and expert in a field of your choice.

Do not let one setback, mistake or failure hold you back. After a disastrous public speaking engagement, it can be tempting to avoid that in the future but as Jaz suggested, failure should be viewed as another opportunity to learn, reflect and improve.

Endnote

1 https://twitter.com/dylanwiliam/status/1571954811234586624.

7 Social media

Social media has become embedded into most people's daily lives, routines and methods of communication. It was once considered a platform for personal connections, relationships and interests but has developed to become a powerful professional tool. Businesses and individuals use social media to share, promote and market content they create. Social media can be very effective for building engagement through networking, developing connections and gaining an audience of followers. Through these platforms individuals and businesses can build their profile or a brand. Using social media for professional purposes can contribute to additional income and finances.

I am well aware of the role and significance social media has had on my career. It contributes to the reason why I am writing this book. I began sharing content online, outside of my school and work environment. I quickly gained a following and attracted the attention of magazines, publishing houses, event organisers and potential employers. Social media isn't solely responsible for my success but it provided a professional platform for me and continues to do so.

In 2017 I was invited to speak on a discussion panel at the BETT Abu Dhabi, Middle East conference. The focus of the panel discussion was '*How social media platforms can contribute to teacher's professional development. Methods of using Facebook, Instagram and Twitter to connect with other teachers globally and create a shared knowledge base*'. I have been an advocate for social media for many years, and despite some challenges and frustrations I continue to use it regularly and encourage others to do so. I am a regular user of Twitter, LinkedIn, Facebook and Instagram. I have a YouTube channel that is gradually growing with both subscribers and content. I rarely use Pinterest and do not have accounts with TikTok, Snapchat or Mastodon. Despite my personal preferences, the advice in this chapter about social media is applicable and transferable across the different channels.

There are different features across the varying platforms. Each will have its pros and cons. The key aspects when considering which platform to use are these; firstly, what is the purpose and reason for using social media?, secondly, whom do you wish to connect with online? Twitter and LinkedIn are useful for staying up to date

DOI: 10.4324/9781003380528-8

with news and trends as well as being able to participate in debate and discussion with a large professional network. Instagram and Pinterest are more visual apps for viewing or sharing content such as classroom displays, lesson ideas, resources and quotes for inspiration and motivation. YouTube and TikTok allow users to view and upload video content. Facebook can include a range of the features above and can be useful for joining specific online communities.

Teachers new to the profession use their initiative or are encouraged by others to find social media channels which can offer support, ideas, inspiration and more. For many experienced teachers and leaders, me included, this is not something we have had access to throughout our careers. It is difficult to access data regarding the number of users in education that use social media for professional purposes.

Throughout this chapter I won't focus on specific aspects, for example, features and functions of the various apps and websites, because social media is continually evolving and changing. Users of social media channels have to quickly adapt when a new feature is added or removed. I won't recommend specific individuals to follow as these would simply be my personal recommendations and they may not be fitting for everyone. A benefit of social media is the ability to curate content and decide whom to follow. This can be based on your interests, your current role or deciding who you might want to be part of your professional network.

The UK Social Media Statistics 2022, published in February 2022, noted: '*There are **4.6 billion** social media users around the world. This number represents 58% of the global population. Although it's worth noting that "users" does not necessarily mean unique individuals*'.[1] In regard to the UK, the published statistics revealed that '*Social media usage in the UK has increased over the last 12 months. In January 2022, 84% of the equivalent of the UK population use social media*', and the average user in the UK spends 1 hour 48 minutes using social media per day.

Another point to consider is that usage can vary considerably. For example, an individual could be an avid user of social media through posting and checking content throughout the day in contrast to someone who may have an account but only uses it occasionally.

The outbreak of Covid-19 changed the daily habits and routines of many individuals, and schooling had to adapt during the pandemic lockdown. Unsurprisingly, the data published revealed '*Since January 2021, active social media usage has increased by 10%, or 424 million users. This is a significant rise considering the enormous increase in users who joined social media platforms during the early days of the COVID-19 lockdowns in 2020*'.[2]

It was reported that although social media users do use multiple platforms, they will have a particular favourite. The UK Social Media Statistics show TikTok was the most-downloaded mobile app in 2021, but the world's most-used social media platform was Facebook, followed by YouTube and WhatsApp.[3] Facebook, WhatsApp and YouTube all vary considerably in terms of their purpose. Facebook is a networking platform to post updates and stay connected with a community. WhatsApp is a direct messaging service that can be used in both a personal and professional capacity, and YouTube is a global platform for sharing and viewing video content.

There is now an increased awareness of screen time with many people trying to monitor and self-regulate their screen time use. There are educators that do not, and do not intend to, use social media for professional purposes. This is understandable as there can be challenges as a professional, for example, members of the school community finding and following social media accounts of teachers and leaders.

In 2022 there were several reports of teachers experiencing abuse and harassment via TikTok videos targeting teachers. The footage and photos of teachers were used without consent. Very serious insults were directed at staff members and posted anonymously. The abuse included homophobic, sexist and racist insults.

The General Secretary of Association of School and College Leaders (ASCL) Geoff Barton told BBC News, 'Social-media platforms should be legally responsible for ensuring they have processes in place which prevent offensive and abusive material from being posted in the first place'. TikTok did respond to these complaints and stated they were taking extra measures to remove videos targeting teachers.[4] Schools have also involved the police in their investigations.

This has the potential to be terrifying as untrue, harmful and defamatory comments and videos posted online can reach a large audience very quickly, causing damage to a professional reputation of the individual targeted as well as the school. Abusive content against educators needs to be taken very seriously and acted on because of the consequences it can have on mental health. Putting up with abuse online, from anyone in the school environment, is not part of the job description and is totally unacceptable.

NASUWT, The Teachers Union addressed this issue on their website with the condemnation of the abuse of teachers online. The statement from NASUWT included the following:

> The NASUWT deplores the abuse of teachers and school or college leaders, including online and through the use of technology. Whilst recent attention has focused on the abuse of teachers via the TikTok platform, it is important to recognise that teachers and school or college leaders are also reporting incidents of online or remote abuse across all leading social media platforms as well as by email, telephone and text messaging of the abuse of teachers online.[5]

All social media platforms have options to report any harassment or abuse. Schools also need to have clear policies in place to educate students and the wider school community about acceptable behaviour online. Support should be in place for any teachers that find themselves victim to online abuse.

Despite the potential problems and challenges with social media, there are many benefits to its professional and personal use. Teacher Tapp provided the following statements to their users in December 2021: 'The benefits of using social media have outweighed the downsides for me'.

The responses illustrated that nearly two-thirds of users agreed it is beneficial to have social media and that the benefits outweigh the negative aspects.[6] Below is an exploration of the potential benefits so that you can ensure, as a social media user, you are reaping the benefits or if you are not using social media this may encourage you to do so.

Professional networking

Social media can be intimidating and overwhelming initially, but once a network is built that can change the overall experience. It can open doors to a wider community of educators beyond your school and workplace. A Professional Learning Community (PLC) or Professional Learning Network (PLN) for many people is the main reason why they use social media. A network of educators and like-minded individuals can offer support, guidance, friendship, inspiration and much more.

Teaching can be difficult, and challenges can range from workload, work related stress, tension with colleagues, behaviour issues in the classroom and more. Talking to trusted friends and colleagues can be helpful, but sometimes it may not be possible to speak to a colleague and friends/family members may not fully understand, especially if they are not part of the teaching profession.

In addition to support, an online professional network and community can provide opportunities for collaboration. This can include the creation and sharing of resources and lesson planning. Another alternative is to collaborate and work on a project that may involve setting up a group, co-authoring an article or organising an event. Collaboration can support teacher workload, lead to new relationships and partnerships and open more doors for professional development and progression.

Relationships online can eventually turn into real life connections with individuals meeting in person, at a conference or event. In addition to learning from others, social media can be a great virtual place to support others too. Communication and interaction are at the heart of social media and it's important to take advantage of this.

Professional development

A network of educators can be a great source of professional development. Educators are regularly sharing content, ideas and advice online and this can be very helpful for teachers new to the profession or those more experienced. Blogs and articles are made accessible through social media, for others to read, learn and reflect on. Users can post questions asking for advice, recommendations or to encourage debate and discussion.

Social media has made it easy and accessible for educators to keep up to date with the latest development, policy changes and stories relevant to education. There are many professional development courses and events that can be costly but social media can offer a daily source of professional learning that is free (or low cost, if you choose to upgrade to extra social media features and functions). It is low cost, accessible and flexible in terms of when you wish to engage and what you wish to focus on.

Educators can use social media to reflect on their practice and leadership. This can be done through writing posts or threads (a thread is a series of posts linked together, to enable users to go beyond the 240-character limit). If the reflections don't reveal personal information about students or include anything that could damage the professional reputation of the individual or school, they can be useful for promoting discussion and dialogue too.

Sharing content to a global audience

If you are planning on creating and sharing content, for example, lesson resources, blogs, articles or books, then social media is an essential marketing and promotional tool. Using social media to share and promote blog posts will very likely lead to increased traffic, engagement and direction to your website.

If you want to become an established keynote speaker then a social media profile and presence is necessary. A profile will likely lead to invitations and requests to speak at events. If you want to reach an audience wider than your school community, social media will enable that to happen.

If you are seeking honest feedback and critique, you are likely to find this online! Comments are not always constructive and kind but those individuals can be blocked and removed. However, sharing content with a large audience will result in many of your followers liking the content you share and find it useful but there will also be vocal users with their opinions and opposition. This can be challenging but it can also be helpful for reflection and professional learning.

Building a brand can appear to sound corporate but many individuals in education are doing this and have done so successfully.

Influencers in education

Social media influencers have grown in popularity and prominence in recent years. Many celebrities use their fame to become influencers, and by doing so they promote products, brands and earn a lot of money. There are influencers who have gained their large followings through social media and there are influencers in a range of fields.

Being an influencer will bring many benefits including a large following, having an online presence and earning a profile. There can be extra benefits which can include receiving free products, privileges and perks, in addition to gaining recognition in a particular field. There are also negative aspects of being an influencer, for example, the higher the follower count the likelihood of negative comments and online trolling can increase. It can be very demanding and competitive being an influencer. There can be an expectation for influencers to consistently share content and posts which can be very time consuming.

Influencers can be known for sharing their fashion advice, makeup tutorials, household hacks, gaming reviews, celebrity commentary and much more. There are also student influencers known as 'study tubers'. They have gained a large audience of young followers through sharing study advice and general tips.

In education there are influencers that have a large following, share their views, opinions and commentary on education. They also share and promote content they create and/or content from other individuals, businesses or organisations. Follower count is important, but it is not the only determining factor in regards to whether someone can be viewed as an online influencer in their field. Engagement is crucial. Posting content that people don't view, comment, like or share won't have the intended impact.

Interview with Danielle Compton

Bio: Dani Compton is an experienced classroom teacher from the North West of England. Dani spent the first four years of her career teaching various subjects in secondary schools. In 2020 Dani ventured into the world of further education. She currently teaches GCSE English Language and functional skills English at a college in Merseyside. Dani is also the digital guru for her department and leads her team in using technology in the classroom.

In 2020 Dani started an Instagram account to share best practice as well as offer wellbeing support and advice for teachers. Dani is dedicated to always adapting her teaching and is very passionate about supporting staff and students with mental health advice. You can find Dani on Instagram @mrscompton_ and Twitter @_Mrscompton.

Q1. When did you join social media, in a professional capacity, and why?

I joined social media professionally via Twitter in 2017 during my PGCE to make connections with other teachers and share subject knowledge and pedagogy. I was able to gain so much valuable knowledge from Twitter in the form of resources and learning from experienced teachers and leaders. In 2020 I made an Instagram page to further share my ideas and thoughts on teaching. This is where I found an incredible community of teachers from across the globe covering primary to further education. I decided to join as I was frankly bored during lockdown and used it to top up my professional development and share my own teaching experiences.

Q2. What social media platform (or platforms) do you use most and why?

Twitter and Instagram are my main platforms I use, as they are the best for finding quick tips and tricks. Instagram is my favourite as their reels feature shows how teachers may do certain things in a classroom. I find the Instagram community more positive and supportive than other platforms. I have used Facebook occasionally to discuss ideas with other teachers and to share resources. I found this particularly valuable when I was in a department that wasn't as secure and didn't have a solid foundation for subject knowledge.

Q3. What benefits have you found from using social media?

I have benefited from being able to find a plethora of resources to use and see how other teachers have used forms of pedagogy in their lessons. Seeing other teachers' resources has been a game changer as it's given me so many new avenues to trial with my learners. The broad connections have also been another great benefit as I now have access to a hive mind of incredible teachers ready to give advice and support whenever I need it.

I have also gained many CPD opportunities that I would never have known about if I hadn't made use of Twitter and Instagram. Much of this CPD has been from other teachers sharing their best practice and is very precise so it never feels like a waste as I've been interested in that topic rather than being told what CPD I am doing.

Q4. Have you experienced any challenges using social media?

The main challenge using social media is the negativity that comes out of some users. Social media can be a very positive place the majority of the time, however, there are a minority of users who can be harsh in their critiques or state their opinions in a rude way. This in turn can lead to arguments or heated debates which I tend to see more on Twitter and Facebook and I avoid at all costs! Instagram, in my experience, is the most supportive and celebratory which is what attracts me to it.

Secondly, comparing yourself to other teachers can be hard not to do, it's only natural. It's important to remember that people mainly share the best parts of their practice online and rarely their failures. Teachers all have different contexts and settings and so it is never helpful to compare your classroom, teaching or marking to others.

Q5. Do you have any advice for someone wanting to use social media to share content?

Just go for it! You can share as much or as little as you want. You can be anonymous or not – it's completely up to you. Don't be pressured into posting all the time or worrying about followers and what other teachers are doing. Just be authentic in what you post. I share a variety of things I think might benefit other teachers, from advice on toxic school environments to a new work outfit. Teaching can sometimes be a lonely profession so sharing your lessons, resources or just general opinions can be so helpful. When sharing content online, just be sure to really check over what you are sharing, as the nature of the job can be sensitive. Give a couple of platforms a try and see which one you find best; you may find negative users but the block button is always there if needed!

Q6. Do you feel social media has empowered you professionally and/or personally, and if so, why?

Social media has certainly empowered me professionally. When I started my account in April 2020, I was not in a good place professionally or personally. My confidence in regard to teaching was at rock bottom after a tumultuous time in a toxic environment. Starting my Instagram account saved my teaching career in many ways as I was ready to walk away from teaching altogether. But the supportive community brought me back and gave me the confidence to get a new job and get back in the classroom.

After sharing my own advice and thoughts on teaching, I developed a CPD series designed to support PGCE students and ECT's as some hadn't had the opportunity for CPD and to gain knowledge from teachers in a school due to the pandemic. This gave me massive gains professionally as I would have never thought I could write my own CPD courses, I felt much more confident in my own practices and knew how to justify what I was doing and why.

I have also been able to connect with other educators and reach out to people online if I want advice or need guidance on specific parts of the profession. Social media has led to great opportunities such as being asked to speak at webinars, trial new products, review books and now contributing to this amazing book! Having a wide range of educators at my fingertips has proved vital at times whether it has been for support, to discuss ideas or learn new classroom hacks! The online teaching community has given me so much and I try constantly to give back and be the same connection for other teachers.

Thank you to Danni for sharing her reflective thoughts and experience of using social media professionally.

Advice to gain followers and connections

A desire for more online followers may appear on the surface as shallow but there are numerous benefits to having a large following and network. Content creators, whether that is someone sharing a classroom idea, resource, blog, article or book will want to reach a large audience. This is easier to do when there is a large social media following. I have gained over 55,000 followers on Twitter. My Twitter follower count is continually and gradually increasing. This has taken time and is a result of the posts I share on a regular basis focusing on teaching and learning in the classroom.

Content can include opinion posts, for example, there are people in education that regularly share and comment on the latest developments and news in education. I find their accounts interesting; they help me to stay informed and can provide a wide range of views and opinions. Other social media content shared by teachers include classroom resources, ideas and general guidance to support pedagogy and improve practice. Content can involve sharing advice in a specific area of education or producing content through infographics, videos, written material or podcasts.

In addition to posting opinions and content, it is important to share, promote and celebrate the work of others. This can include an article written by someone else that you would recommend or a specific classroom idea that could benefit another teacher online. Social media is an online community and through championing others a camaraderie can develop.

When I present at an event or an online webinar, I ensure my social media contact details are visible on my opening and closing slide. I encourage people to follow me and stay in touch online. This does increase followers but it can also continue a conversation, provide an opportunity to receive feedback and expand my professional network. Although some individuals may be reluctant to promote their social media accounts, there is nothing wrong with asking or encouraging others to follow, connect or subscribe.

I also ask my followers to retweet or share my posts if I want it to reach a larger audience or if I am seeking advice, guidance or feedback. In return when others ask for a post to be shared outside of their network of followers, I do so (if the content is appropriate). I use social media to promote my books and I will regularly ask followers to post a photo of my book if they have a copy. I take a huge amount of satisfaction and pride from this, seeing my book in the hands of readers. This also helps to promote and generate interest in my books and therefore can lead to an increase in readers and sales.

Spotlight: Ross Morrison McGill a.k.a. Teacher Toolkit

Ross Morrison McGill founded the Twitter account @TeacherToolkit in 2010 and he is one of the most followed educators on social media in the world. In 2015, he was nominated as one of the '500 Most Influential People in Britain' by *The Sunday Times*. He remains the only classroom teacher to feature to this day on that list.

Through sharing resources and ideas online, Ross has built his website, www.teachertoolkit.co.uk, described as one of the 'most influential blogs on education in the UK', winning a UK Blog Award and reaching over 17 million readers! Ross started teaching in 1991, he was a school leader for twenty years and worked in some of the most challenging secondary schools in London. Today, he works with pupils, teachers and school leaders across the world, supporting teaching and learning, workload and teacher mental health.

Ross offers the following advice to educators to increase their profile online and grow an audience:[7]

1. Have a simple Twitter handle, easy to recall and identify

2. Create a clear personalised logo that remains on your profile

3. Use the same name and logo across other social media platforms

4. Push out professional content, so users know what to expect

5. Be consistent.

Ross regularly collaborates with and supports female educators through his website, blogs and co-authoring books. Ross co-authored *The revision revolution: How to build a culture of effective study in your school* (2022) with Helen Howell, *60 second CPD* (2020) with Hannah Beech, *Toxic schools* (2018) with Dr Helen Woodley, and *Hairdresser or footballer: Bridging the gender gap in schools* (2018) with Holly Anderton. Ross is currently working on an upcoming book with Julie Keyes, *A guide to coaching*.

Throughout my career, as it has evolved and changed from classroom teacher to author and education consultant, Ross has offered very helpful advice and guidance. I have always appreciated his kindness and he is someone in education I admire. Ross is an example of a successful man in education that is keen to support and empower others in education and recognises that more needs to be done to give women the platform they deserve.

Staying safe online

Digital safety is of paramount importance and relevant for children and adults. This section includes discussion of distressing topics, including harassment and transphobia.

Women aiming to use social media for personal and professional reasons can find themselves victim to online sexual harassment. Sexual harassment exists in the workplace through sexist, misogynistic and inappropriate comments and behaviour. Those behaviours and attitudes can occur online but abusers can be hidden through anonymity and they can be unknown to the victim.

Rights of Women is a women's rights registered charity offering legal support to women. Their website states:

Our women lawyers provide free specialist legal advice to women survivors because we recognise that women do not have fair and equal access to the law. Our policy and campaigning work is based on what we learn from the women we advise. It is aimed at improving the law and legal systems so they deliver better outcomes for women.

A survey conducted by Rights of Women in 2021, during the Covid-19 pandemic, found there had been an increase in online sexual harassment when many women worked from home during this period across England and Wales. The survey reported, *'Nearly 1 in 2 women who have experienced sexual harassment at work reported to experience some to all of it online'.*[8] Further findings from the study reveal, *'45% of women experiencing sexual harassment, reported experiencing the harassment remotely. Remote sexual harassment refers to the following: sexual messages (e.g. email, texts, social media); cyber harassment (e.g. via Zoom, Teams, Slack etc); and sexual calls'.*[9] The report added, *'72% of women experiencing sexual harassment at work do not feel their employer is doing enough to protect and/or support them from the harassment and abuse'.* The report is not specifically focused on one profession but offers a wider account of women in the workplace.

There have been numerous documentaries and reports focusing on women's safety online ranging from revenge pornography (a private video of explicit and sexual act being shared online without consent) to sexual harassment and more specifically cyber flashing. Cyber flashing involves sending an unsolicited sexual image. Cyber flashing can be done through social media platforms, Bluetooth devices such as Airdrop or messaging services. The government in England announced in March 2022, *'"Cyberflashing" will become a new criminal offence with perpetrators facing up to two years behind bars under new laws to be introduced by the Government'.*[10]

Online abuse is an umbrella term that can include a wide range of actions and behaviours that cause distress, harm or trauma to an individual. Online abuse can include stalking, name calling and trolling, hate speech and physical threats of violence. Reports and statistics will never show a truly accurate account of online abuse because not all online abuse is reported.

In 2019 the BBC published 'Transgender people treated "inhumanely" online'. This report shared research illustrating the abuse transgender individuals can experience online. This included a range of targeted transphobic insults and slurs. According to the TransActual Trans Lives Survey (2021), *'99% of trans people surveyed have experienced transphobia on social media'.*[11] This highlights how transwomen can be vulnerable online and action should be taken to prevent transphobic abuse. Chapter 8 focuses on how we can support and empower women; this naturally includes transwomen too.

I have trans friends and family members, and being an ally to the trans community is something I am continually learning to do. Initially, I knew very little about the language, terminology and experiences linked to the trans community. If you are unsure how you can support transwomen and the wider trans community there is some advice below as a useful starting point.

- **Avoid 'dead naming'.** This refers to calling a trans person by their previous name, a name they no longer use or identify with. This can be distressing.

- **Pronouns.** Respecting the pronouns people use and including your pronouns to show how you identify can show support to the trans community. If unsure of someone's pronouns, ask and if the wrong pronouns are used, apologise and use the correct pronouns in the future.

- **Don't gossip with others or speculate about a transgender individual.** Do not assume someone is transgender based on their appearance. Avoid compliments or comments that focus attention on being trans, for example *'You actually look feminine'*.

- **Don't make jokes about the transgender community.** This is a sensitive area and jokes might be used as an attempt to 'break the ice' or lead to banter but it can cause upset and distress.

- **Take time to become educated.** This can be through conversations with members of the trans community (with sensitivity) or further reading. No one has all the answers, and every trans individual is unique but willingness to learn and a desire to be an ally are great signs of support.

- **Kindness is key.**

Women's Aid, a charity organisation to support women and children against domestic violence, published their research which found, *'For 85% of respondents the abuse they received online from a partner or ex-partner was part of a pattern of abuse they also experienced offline'*. Women's Aid added, *'We know that perpetrators of domestic abuse often use online tools to abuse their victims'* (there is further discussion of domestic violence and how to support women in Chapter 8).

There are many benefits to working online from home or using social media professionally but there are also serious e-safety concerns. Social media and video conference platforms do have policies and procedures in place to keep users safe. These include the ability to set an account to private, not allow people to send direct messages unless they are a confirmed contact, and video conferencing will provide a wait room feature to allow the host to make the decision to let users enter or remove a user. Despite these security features, sexual harassment online can still occur. Women are able to block and report, but prevention would be much more effective and remove the trauma and distress many women have to experience.

Other ways to stay safe online include:

- Never share or keep a record of passwords. Aim for a very unique yet memorable password and use different passwords for different websites.

- Set up login authentication and verification. Most websites and social media apps have this function (it can be found in the security and privacy settings). This safety feature requires the user to verify they have logged in when they login from a new device. They verify this by using their mobile phone number or email address and will receive a code to prove they are the user attempting to login.

- Invest in anti-virus software and seek support if unsure how to do so.

- If using an account visible to the public, be mindful of content shared, for example, personal photos or location sharing. Many people do post photos, which is a significant aspect of social media, but ensure consent is granted from all those in the photos and consider if the photos were to be viewed by students, colleagues and current or future employer would that be an issue or concern?

- It is important to continually be aware of a digital footpath and information that is available publicly.

Aim to build a positive and powerful professional community and network. This can be achieved through carefully selecting whom to follow, engage and connect with. Social media can offer a community that provides support, friendship, advice, inspiration and much more, but it is up to the social media user to curate and control this as best they can.

Social media links to many of the ways women can be empowered in education. Through social media women can gain a supportive and collaborative network of like-minded educators. Women can champion, promote and empower other women through social media. Female writers, from bloggers to authors, will need social media to ensure their published content reaches a wide audience of readers. Social media can also be an excellent source of professional development, learning and reflection for classroom teachers and school leaders

It is vital women are safe online. There are steps women can take to stay safe, but all websites and social media platforms have a responsibility to protect women online. Social media has transformed my career and provided opportunities for me to embrace and enjoy. This is true of many other women, especially those featured in this book, and can open doors to empower women in education.

Endnotes

1 https://www.avocadosocial.com/uk-social-media-statistics-2022/.
2 https://www.avocadosocial.com/uk-social-media-statistics-2022/.
3 https://www.avocadosocial.com/uk-social-media-statistics-2022/.
4 https://www.bbc.co.uk/news/education-59264238.
5 https://www.nasuwt.org.uk/advice/health-safety/social-media-and-online-abuse-of-teachers.html.
6 https://teachertapp.co.uk/articles/curriculum-intent-social-media-regulation-and-the-teacher-tapp-upgrade/.
7 https://www.teachertoolkit.co.uk/2015/07/02/20-social-media-tips-for-teachers-by-teachertoolkit/.
8 https://rightsofwomen.org.uk/news/rights-of-women-survey-reveals-online-sexual-harassment-has-increased-as-women-continue-to-suffer-sexual-harassment-whilst-working-through-the-covid-19-pandemic/.
9 https://rightsofwomen.org.uk/news/rights-of-women-survey-reveals-online-sexual-harassment-has-increased-as-women-continue-to-suffer-sexual-harassment-whilst-working-through-the-covid-19-pandemic/.
10 https://www.gov.uk/government/news/cyberflashing-to-become-a-criminal-offence.
11 https://www.transactual.org.uk/trans-lives-21.

8 Supporting and empowering women in education

To support women in education is to empower women, and everyone plays an important role towards achieving this goal. Women have to be bold and take steps for themselves. Those steps can include applying for a new job or promotion, volunteering to lead professional development or deciding to try something new like writing a blog or launching a podcast. Initiative and ambition aren't always enough. A supportive, understanding and inclusive work environment and network is vital for the empowerment of women.

Former Prime Minister of New Zealand Jacinda Ardern received worldwide attention when she became the youngest female head of government in the world, elected as prime minister in 2017 at age 37. Ardern has become known as an advocate for empathetic leadership. During her time in office she endured sexist remarks and inappropriate questions from the media and public. During her tenure, Ardern gave birth to a child and had to lead through national crises including a natural disaster, terrorist attacks and the global Covid-19 pandemic.

Ardern has been quoted with the following when discussing critique of her leadership style:

One of the criticisms I've faced over the years is that I'm not aggressive enough or assertive enough, or maybe somehow, because I'm empathetic, it means I'm weak. I totally rebel against that. I refuse to believe that you cannot be both compassionate and strong.

Many women in the workplace can relate to similar criticisms. Examples of this include describing a woman as bossy when she is being decisive or assertive. Another is to describe a woman as emotional when demonstrating passion and enthusiasm. When women voice their concerns or objections, this can be described as argumentative. These approaches and narratives are outdated and need to be challenged by everyone.

It is important at this point to warn readers that throughout this chapter there are references to sensitive topics including suicide, bereavement, miscarriage,

DOI: 10.4324/9781003380528-9

violence and abuse against women. At the end of this chapter are a list of resources providing support and guidance to anyone experiencing distress.

During the process of writing this book I used different social media platforms to ask the question:

What challenges do women experience in the workplace that are unique to women?

Below is a summary of the different responses (all anonymised and the responses were from men and women):

- The motherhood penalty (discussed later in this chapter). This refers to the negative impact having children can have on the career of a woman. False assumptions can be made, that a mother is not fully invested in her career, less committed, competent or focused. This also includes parental discrimination.

- There are challenges with balancing workload and parental responsibilities, although this does not seem to impact men in the same way when they have children. Feeling torn or guilty because time has to be divided between personal and professional commitments.

- Pregnancy discrimination. This can include being overlooked for promotion before, during or after maternity leave. Experiencing negative biases, for example, a preconception that a pregnant woman or new mother is no longer as dedicated to their work.

- Hormonal challenges not being understood ranging from periods, fertility, pregnancy and menopause. These topics are often avoided or ignored in the workplace despite their importance and impact.

- Sexual harassment is not always tackled. It can include inappropriate comments and/or behaviour from students or colleagues.

- Women being perceived as being competitive or selfish when showing ambition.

- Other women can be hostile to women by demonstrating professional jealousy or unpleasant traits.

Kindness is key

After announcing her resignation as Prime Minister of New Zealand, Ardern was asked how she would like to be remembered as a leader and her response was *'as someone who always tried to be kind'*.[1] Kindness is an important quality in a leader or classroom teacher. Kindness is also at the heart of being supportive and empowering others. 'Be Kind' is a phrase and hashtag that has grown in popularity over recent years, although the idea and concept of being kind is far from new or innovative.

It seems so blindingly obvious we should be kind to each other and ourselves. Yet, there is still a need to promote and demonstrate kindness whether that's online due to the increased use of social media platforms and subsequent trolling, or in real life situations from the playground, classroom, to all walks of adult life, including the staffroom.

One barrier to the Be Kind movement is that people naturally have different interpretations of kindness. Unconsciously, we might select to whom we are kind to and when. Kindness is defined in the Oxford English dictionary as '*the quality of being friendly, generous and considerate*'. Kindness embodies all of those qualities plus much more. I believe that at the heart of kindness is being genuine. Kind actions shouldn't be motivated by factors such as pleasing or impressing others or out of guilt or pressure, but the genuine desire to be kind to another person as well as to be kind to ourselves.

Dr David Hamilton has carried out a significant amount of research and authored books focused on the physical and mental benefits of kindness. Hamilton defines kindness as '*an honest, heartfelt expression. It can be a thought, a word or an act that is motivated by a desire to help*'.[2] Kindness and helping others are intertwined and connected, in the same way kindness is directly linked to happiness. Helping others is kindness and being kind often (not always) leads to happiness.

There are many misconceptions around kindness, for example, the idea of being a push-over or never saying no to anyone or any request. Kindness isn't a weakness yet many people known for their kindness can be viewed negatively as not being able to have difficult conversations or lacking the ability to lead. Being kind to those that aren't kind to us requires strength and courage to do so. Factors can influence our behaviour including stress, exhaustion, hormones and relationships, so is it even possible to be kind **all** of the time or is that simply unrealistic? Should we aim to be **kinder?**

On 15 February 2020, television presenter and celebrity Caroline Flack tragically took her own life, aged 40. The *Strictly Come Dancing* champion and former host of the reality show *Love Island* struggled with mental health as well as other personal issues that only she and the people close to her were fully aware of, despite the media documenting many aspects of her life. There was also the treatment and scrutiny she experienced by the national press with many arguing her suicide was death by the media. It has been suggested there was more media intrusion because of her gender. Others argue that media intrusion and reporting is part of the package when people seek fame but where is the line drawn?

Prior to her death, Flack posted an image on social media of a widely shared quote, '*In a world where you can be anything, be kind*'. After her death, this post was flooded with comments from her friends and followers online. This led to the hashtag #BeKind to trend and eventually t-shirts and other items of clothing and merchandise displaying the Be Kind phrase appeared. The phrase and movement Be Kind existed prior to this but it has become more prevalent in the UK since the death of Caroline Flack. The idea and premise behind #BeKind are lovely.

Promoting a society filled with kindness, but how does this shift from being a hashtag to a reality?

Recent years have been eventful and distressing with global events impacting everyone. The Covid-19 pandemic put extra pressure and strain on children and adults. The murder of George Floyd in the US has highlighted the racial injustices and divisions within society that need healing. Violence against women and misogyny have been commonplace in the news. It seems a very apt time to promote kindness towards one another.

There have been times when I could and should have been much kinder. I am only human and regretfully, I have made mistakes. I reflect on my experiences, trying to learn and do differently or better. I have experienced many challenges in my attempts to become a kinder person, both in my personal and professional life.

People often say being kind is easy. The concept is simple but we can be put in very challenging, tested and tense situations and/or be faced with difficult or aggressive people who stir up various emotions and make being kind very tough at times. Women, as demonstrated throughout this book, can be faced with unique challenges. Kindness, support and encouragement from others can certainly make a difference.

Many teachers have considered leaving teaching or have left the profession because they worked in a school environment that lacked kindness, support, empathy or understanding, especially at times in their life when these were needed most. Children need to be surrounded by kindness and support but adults do too. The #WomenEd movement has inspired women in education by encouraging them to be 10% braver. Everyone in education has the potential to be 10% kinder. Kindness isn't about a one-off gesture, it's how we behave day in and day out.

Being kind and supportive of others will ultimately help and empower them, but there are other benefits to this. Are you familiar with the 'helper's high'? It is likely you have experienced the 'helper's high' yourself. It's the warm feeling of elation and happiness we feel when we help others. According to *Psychology Today*:

> *Any kind act, statement or behaviour that is simply about intentionally doing something nice that impacts your family, others, your community, the environment and the world in a positive way, matters. The more we practise doing nice things, the better we get at it. When we practise kindness, we're training our brains to get better at kindness as the brain learns that we want to think about being nice. When we help others and do kind acts, it causes our brain to release endorphins, the chemicals that give us feelings of fervour and high spirits – similar to a "runner's high." Doing something nice for someone also gives the brain a serotonin boost, the chemical that gives us that feeling of satisfaction and well-being.*[3]

Being kind simply makes us feel physically and emotionally good. This could be argued to be a selfish motivation for kindness, to make us feel better, but it is not selfish. If kindness makes us feel positive and happy, then that is simply an added bonus! In addition to the 'helper's high', research has indicated that the act of being kind can contribute to reducing anxiety and stress, although no one is claiming this is a miracle silver bullet cure for stress (silver bullets don't exist in education and life).

The results of a study on happiness from the University of British Columbia (UBC) explained that, *'social anxiety is associated with low positive affect (PA), a factor that can significantly affect psychological well-being and adaptive functioning'*. Positive affect refers to an individual's experience of positive moods such as joy, interest, enthusiasm and alertness. The researchers at UBC found that the participants who engaged in acts of kindness displayed significant increases in PA that were sustained over the four weeks of the study.[4]

Mark Kelly promised the audience at his TEDx Talk that he could share with them the secret to a longer and happier life where we can all look and feel better. The title of his presentation shares the answer: *'How one act of kindness a day can change your life'*. Kelly shared his personal story of how one day he randomly decided to purchase a cup of coffee for a homeless man whilst he was on his way to work. That day, he felt good about his small act of kindness. He explained how he attended yoga classes and read various self-help books in his quest to feel better, but nothing quite made him feel as good as helping others. He continued to help others by creating care packages that he would carry around and give to people who needed them. His act of kindness may even simply be to wait to hold the door open for another person. Kelly was experiencing the helper's high and it became addictive.

One day his colleagues noticed his mood and actions and they enquired about his acts of kindness. After explaining helping others was actually making him feel really positive and good, his workplace decided to implement this too. Staff would carry out random acts of kindness for one another. The acts of kindness included buying someone a coffee or surprising a colleague by cleaning their car. One employee had her bike stolen, and each of her colleagues made a small donation that managed to cover the cost of a new bike. She was so overwhelmed by their kindness she cried with gratitude. Being kind has become an integral aspect of his workplace and has changed his life and the lives of his colleagues for the better. In his TEDx Talk Kelly goes on to explore the health benefits of being kind, such as a reduction in anxiety levels. Blood pressure can be reduced, and blood circulation can increase. Kelly argues that even if we undertake acts of kindness for ourselves, we help society in doing so.

Being kind is often contagious. An act of kindness or even a smile can inspire others to do the same. For teachers and school leaders the concept of kindness being infectious is incredibly powerful because schools are places where people interact daily. We can model kindness and inspire others to be kind.

Toxic schools exist. This isn't a secret, and although still considered a taboo topic it is becoming more open to debate and discussion due to the presence of teachers' online tweeting, writing blogs and articles for educational magazines. Teachers are publicly (at times anonymously due to the potential implications) calling out these toxic school environments by sharing their experiences and offering advice for others who may not be enjoying their experience as a teacher.

Schools can be viewed as toxic based on the whole school culture, policies or approach to workload and wellbeing (or lack of consideration and recognition of these issues). Toxic cultures can be within departments or groups within schools. This toxicity brings lots of issues for the teachers and leaders to ultimately try to change and improve the environment for all. Toxic school environments often lack kindness. You may currently work in a toxic school, have left one previously or unfortunately find yourself in that environment in the future.

If Be Kind is a bandwagon, then some schools have certainly jumped on it. Schools and leaders can use their school website or social media pages to declare they promote kindness, posting photos of happy children and cakes in the staffroom (both of which are undeniably lovely!) but what really needs to be done to create a culture of kindness? What does this day-to-day culture look like? How can a school ensure all staff feel supported and empowered?

When it comes to creating a culture in any work environment, the vision has to be driven from the top, led by example and every individual needs to contribute, otherwise the desired culture won't exist. When there is an appropriate culture of kindness and support, we can all flourish, thrive, feel supported, motivated and empowered.

Supporting female BAME educators

The term BAME (Black, Asian and ethnic minority) for individuals is widely used, but the government in England no longer uses the label BAME when referring to different ethnic minority groups in society. The differences between ethnic minorities is one of the reasons cited for this change. The Civil Service blog explained, *'"BAME" is a catch-all term, frequently used to group all ethnic minorities together. This can disguise huge differences in outcomes between ethnic groups. For example, we know that the picture of educational achievement across different ethnic groups is complex'.*[5] However, as this term is still currently used widely I have included it in this book.

In 2020, *The Guardian* reported, *'Almost half of all schools in England have no black or minority ethnic teachers, and even where there is diversity among staff, senior leadership teams are invariably white, research has found'.*[6] The article added, *'As a result, minority ethnic pupils can go through school without seeing their background represented in their teachers'.* Teaching staff and leadership in schools should be reflective of the society we live in. In addition to the discussion around the lack of female leaders in education, the promotion of BAME school leaders must also be encouraged.

The BAMEed Network was founded in 2017 as a grassroot registered charity in the UK run by a team of educators. BAMEed aims to make the education sector more representative of society. The organisation encourages more BAME representation in schools and school leadership. BAMEed Network now has regional hubs across the UK to promote networking, collaboration and share awareness of the need for more BAME educators and leaders in schools. BAMEed also offers support to BAME educators experiencing discrimination and challenges. They also offer support and guidance to schools to understand anti-racism, diversity, equality and inclusion (DEI) in the workplace.

To find out more about BAMEed you can visit the website https://www.bameednetwork.com and follow the social media account @BAMEEdNetwork on Twitter.

Pregnancy and motherhood

Although there are common symptoms pregnant women experience, every mother to be will have their own unique experience of pregnancy. For some, pregnancy is very straightforward with little or no symptoms in the early trimester and the pregnancy itself can go smoothly as planned. Other women may experience very severe symptoms with intense morning sickness, tiredness, swollen breasts, constipation or other symptoms. Support for women in the workplace during pregnancy is essential.

The Gov.uk website clearly explains and defines pregnant employees' legal rights, and it is important to be aware of these. They include:

● paid time off for antenatal care

● maternity leave

● maternity pay or maternity allowance

● protection against unfair treatment, discrimination or dismissal.

There is further information on the website about pregnancy and maternity discrimination, health and safety, maternity leave and more.[7] Despite this legislation there are many examples of where women have felt or experienced discrimination. Legislation will vary internationally. Some countries are more progressive and supportive than others, but again it is vital to be aware of and understand the legal rights.

For pregnant women at work, there are several ways in which schools can support expectant mothers, in addition to merely legislative entitlements. Below are some approaches that schools have adopted:

● Covering extra responsibilities such as lunch or break duty. This can help reduce the travel around the school site, benefitting women during the later stages of pregnancy. This can also ensure time for a toilet break, more often required by pregnant women.

- Designating a parking space for pregnant women close to the school entrance or their classroom.

- Considering workload implications and offering flexibility where possible. For example, changes can be put in place for attending a parents evening online, in contrast to staying late in the school building.

- Lunch time must always be protected to ensure pregnant mothers can eat and hydrate (this is relevant to all members of staff). They should not be expected to run a club, host a detention or any other demanding activity during this time, unless they are comfortable and it is safe to do so.

Pregnant women, often for reasons unknown, can suffer the devastating loss of a baby. Miscarriage is more likely to occur during the first trimester or the first twenty-three weeks of pregnancy. The early stages of pregnancy can be a very daunting time for a woman as they will be aware of the increased risk. According to the NHS website, *'Miscarriages are much more common than most people realise. Among people who know they're pregnant, it's estimated about 1 in 8 pregnancies will end in miscarriage'.*[8]

A miscarriage can have a physical and emotional impact on a woman (as well as a man preparing to become a father), and the recommended guidance for absence to recover will vary depending on each individual. To find out about the maternity rights you are entitled to it is worth familiarising yourself with the school policy and union documentation. These can vary based on your employment contract or country of residence. Support, kindness and understanding are vital during this difficult time.

Throughout my career, but especially after I turned 30, I resented comments from other women that suggested they were better teachers because they were mothers. I was told being a parent gave unique insight and understanding of children, one that those without children could not possess or understand. Comments implying someone is a less effective teacher because they do not have children are cruel and unnecessary.

This is a debate I have observed on social media and it is not a constructive discussion. There will be female teachers that struggle or cannot conceive and there will be others who do not wish to have children. The women who do not have or want children are often asked questions about their plans or reasons for this. This is a private and personal decision. Women should not have to justify the life choices they have made.

There is also the 'motherhood penalty' where women experience professional setbacks after having children. Negative comments can be targeted at women with children in the workplace. These comments can infer a female teacher or school leader isn't as committed or dedicated to their role because their children are their priority. This is also very unfair and unkind.

Joeli Brearley is the author of *The motherhood penalty: How to stop motherhood being the kiss of death for your career* (2021). Brearley also founded Pregnant Then Screwed (2015) after losing her job when she was four months pregnant. Brearley writes, *'Choice is a mythical unicorn to mothers. Instead a mother must make decisions within a very constrained framework, choosing between the only possible option for financial and mental survival, and total pandemonium'.*[9]

Brearley explores the many challenges women with children experience adding:

> *A mother's choices are limited by extortionately priced, inflexible, inaccessible childcare. A mother's choices are limited by maternity pay that is well below the national living wage. A mother's choices are limited by the rising cost of living, which means most families need two incomes to cover their basic costs. A mother's choices are limited by a severe lack of part-time jobs and a working culture that demands long hours.*[10]

These are important topics that need to be discussed at a national and regional level in addition to the context of teaching and working in education.

After announcing my pregnancy publicly, there were lots of lovely best wishes and congratulations but there were also some comments I did not appreciate. There were suggestions I would not write any more books or attend conferences or deliver CPD once my child was born. This is untrue.

I will take time during maternity leave to be with my baby, but I have career ambitions. People have assumed I would stay at home to look after our child, no one has assumed or asked if my male partner would do that. There are fathers who take on the primary role of carer when women return to work. However, legislation and paternal pay is designed to support women to look after children as opposed to the father. This is where there needs to be discussion of flexible and part time options in addition to child care considerations.

Spotlight: The Maternity Teacher Paternity Teacher Project (MTPT)

The Maternity Teacher Paternity Teacher Project (MTPT) is a UK registered charity which aims to support parent teachers and offers opportunities for professional development, networking and advice about parental leave. Founded in June 2016 by Emma Sheppard, The MTPT Project has grown and evolved. It is currently run by a team of volunteers and advocates across the UK. The MTPT team includes regional representatives and coaches. There is the option for individual membership which provides access to the members' areas and a wide range of professional learning resources. There is also the option for a school and college membership which includes access to policy templates, consultancy sessions, bespoke training and more.

The MTPT website states:

We believe that parents are entitled to make decisions that support their wellbeing and the wellbeing of their families. Wellbeing means different things for different people: for some, this means maintaining a sense of that 'teacher' identity during the 'break' of parental leave. We think creatively about the type of activities that have a positive impact on our students and can therefore be considered effective professional learning, and we love exploring the simplicity or problem-solving challenge of enjoying these with babies and toddlers. Our community has a significant impact on the culture of schools, influencing organisations to be more equal and more inclusive. The ramifications of our work make teaching not only a family friendly career choice for mothers and fathers, but also improves working conditions for all teachers.[11]

A goal of The MTPT Project, in addition to offering support, is to inspire, empower and connect educators with parental responsibilities. This is a professional network and community that offers a range of services from coffee mornings, blogs, case studies, webinars and training workshops. Research relevant to parent teachers is also published and shared with the aim to raise awareness of the potential challenges and offer solutions and guidance to individuals and schools.

To find out more about The MTPT Project visit the website https://www.mtpt. org.uk/ and follow the social media channels @mtptproject. The MTPT handbook is now available entitled, *A guide to teaching, parenting and creating family friendly schools* (2023).

Misogyny, violence and abuse against women

Empowering and supporting women comes in different forms. It may involve supporting a woman to apply for the job they are considering, or it could mean supporting a female colleague to get through one day at a time because of difficult personal circumstances. One example of this is domestic abuse and violence.

According to the Crime Survey for England and Wales (CSEW), it is estimated that 5.0% of adults aged 16 years and over experienced domestic abuse in the year ending March 2022. CSEW notes that this equates to an estimated 2.4 million adults with 1.7 million women and 699,000 men. The CSEW report also adds, approximately one in five adults aged 16 years and over (10.4 million) had experienced domestic abuse since the age of 16 years. These statistics are based on England and Wales yet domestic abuse occurs across the UK and internationally. Domestic abuse is defined in the Domestic Abuse Act 2021 as: '*Behaviour of a person ("A") towards another person ("B") is "domestic abuse" if — A and B are each aged 16 or over and are personally connected to each other, and the behaviour is abusive.* Behaviour is 'abusive' if it consists of any of the following:

- physical or sexual abuse

- violent or threatening behaviour

- controlling or coercive behaviour.

Other forms of abuse include the economic, psychological or emotional. Abusive behaviour can consist of a single incident or be ongoing. Domestic violence and abuse are not widely discussed within the education sector (certainly not in my experience) outside of annual safeguarding training. However, considering the statistics published (and not all cases of domestic abuse are reported and known), and the fact education is a profession dominated by women, it is a matter of importance and not something to be ignored.

Violence against women is a very serious problem in society. In March 2021, 33-year-old Sarah Everard was reported missing and later found dead. She was walking home one evening, never to make it home. The disappearance led to a large investigation resulting in the discovery of her body. Wayne Couzens, a serving Metropolitan police officer at the time of the disappearance, was charged with her kidnap and murder and later sentenced to life in jail. Unfortunately, this example of brutality and violence against a woman was not a one-off.

In September 2021, Sabina Nessa, a 28-year-old primary school teacher was also attacked and murdered as she was walking home. Koci Selamaj, 36 (someone with a history of violence against women) was arrested and later jailed for life. People held vigils for Sarah Everard and Sabina Nessa to pay their respects to the victims and their families, and also demonstrate condemnation of such horrific violence.

On 5 February 2023, Headteacher Emma Pattison was found dead, alongside her 7-year-old daughter. This was a horrific tragedy, and took place on the school grounds where the family lived. The inquest stated Emma Pattison was shot in the abdomen and chest and her daughter died of a shotgun wound to the head. The police stated the firearm was legally registered to the husband of Emma Pattison.[12] Sky news reported, *'It is believed George Pattison, 39, murdered his wife, Emma Pattison, 45, and their 7-year-old daughter Lettie, before he took his own life'*. There will be further reports published but once again this highlights the dangers women can face.

Case study: Domestic violence experienced by a classroom teacher

Bio: The author of this case study has requested to remain anonymous for both professional and personal reasons.

There are stereotypical tropes about women that experience domestic violence but the harsh reality is domestic violence is universal. Women can be victims of domestic violence regardless of age, race, religion, sexuality, social class or profession. A successful and educated woman can experience domestic violence, and in my experience some people find that difficult to comprehend.

In my late twenties after switching between various jobs, I decided to go back to University to complete a postgraduate certificate in education (PGCE) to become a secondary teacher. I was very excited about this as it had been a career ambition I delayed due to travelling and taking some time to earn and save money. I was accepted onto a course and I managed to secure two placements for the academic year in my local area.

I was surprised how difficult the PGCE course was with lesson planning, marking, reading, assignments and attending lectures. I struggled with the workload and found I had less time for friends, family and my (former) partner. I had been in a relationship with my partner four years prior to starting my PGCE qualification, but it was during this year that problems with him started to become serious.

Despite my disapproval, my partner would take cocaine and smoke cannabis on a regular basis. This was very difficult for me as I am anti-drugs. I was embarking on a new career as a professional and in a position of authority working with children. I worried about the impact his drug use would have on his physical and mental health, but I was also concerned it could harm or ruin my career prospects. This led to many arguments and ongoing tension.

It was during a PGCE placement that my partner hit me for the first time. It was after a night out and he was very drunk. He punched me in the face across my mouth and gave me a split and swollen lip. It was very visible, and I was mortified. The following day my partner sobbed and insisted it would never happen again and he begged me not to end the relationship. I was in love with him, and in the years I had been with him he had never done anything like that so I genuinely believed it was a one-off. I could not face going to school and teaching lessons with my injury visible for everyone to see, I couldn't handle the staring or questions. I took a few days off work and called in sick, and by the time I went back to school I was able to cover any marks with makeup and no questions were asked.

It was the first but not the last time he would hit me. It became a pattern, mainly happening on weekends after drinking, and the pattern also included his tears and pleas to stay with him. It was a relief to have bruises on my arms or thighs because they could be easily covered. At this point my friends and family members all knew what was happening. The attacks didn't just take place behind closed doors. I can recall where he grabbed me around the throat in front of friends until a male friend was able to pull him away from me.

Everyone around me told me I was stupid, pathetic and should leave the relationship, but I just couldn't bring myself to do it. My friends and family were so angry with me, they stopped speaking to me. They thought this would force my hand and help me to leave him, but instead it made me feel like I had no one but him. People around me didn't understand why I stayed in this relationship, but there were things they did not know. During an argument I grabbed my phone to ring for help but he pinched my phone from my hands and destroyed it so I couldn't contact anyone. I had tried to leave him but he had threatened to kill himself or self-harm if I did, and this always shifted guilt onto me. He also made threats to me against my family, warning me that if I left him he would do very bad things to them. This terrified me. I became too scared to leave or suggest ending the relationship.

One morning I received an email from my university mentor addressing all the time off I had during my placement. When there were visible injuries on my face or if I was in too much pain after the physical abuse from my partner I was absent, calling up sick with a different lie each time. My mentor informed me that I was not allowed any more time off because the placement required a certain number of days to be completed in schools to pass the course. If I took more time off I would have to complete the PGCE year again and this could involve another application where my place was not guaranteed.

I was devastated because I could not spend another year training, earning very little money and delaying my career prospects. It was a stressful year I did not wish to repeat. With hindsight I should have told my university advisor the truth, but instead I replied that I understood and there would be no more absences, and there were none.

I begged my partner not to be violent again because my career was at stake. He didn't listen, and following an incident I had to teach lessons with a black eye. I heard children in the corridor mocking me calling me Rocky Balboa and members of staff I didn't know were approaching me, asking what happened. I told a false story about falling over, how it was an accident and it looked much worse than it was, but more injuries followed. People stopped asking questions but the staring increased and it was horrific.

My mentor on the school placement spoke to me privately one day after school and said she was very concerned. I broke down crying and told her about the problems with my partner. She was very quick to judge me and ask why I was still with this man and putting myself at further risk. I tried to tell her I loved him and for many years he wasn't like this but it was alcohol and drugs that changed him. I told her I was also very scared of him and scared to leave him. She was angry with me and said she couldn't help me if I insisted on staying with him. Her tone, looks of disapproval and eye rolling made me feel even lower, which I didn't think was possible.

I completed my PGCE placement and was very fortunate to secure a position for my NQT year at a great school in the local area. After a few weeks at the school

I knew it was a wonderful place to work and it would be a school where I could learn a lot and improve as a teacher with potential for promotion in the future. My partner hadn't been violent for a while so I assumed and hoped that was behind us, but sadly I was wrong.

One evening my partner was angry and took it out on me pushing me around and spitting in my face (something he did a lot). I packed a bag and said it was over. He pushed me to the floor and held a knife to my throat. Again, he warned me if I left him he would kill me and then kill my family by burning their house to the ground. I was so frightened and agreed to stay but I knew I had to get out of the relationship.

The following weekend when my partner was out with his friends I packed all my belongings and had arranged for my Dad to pick me up. I would leave without any drama but I knew there would be trouble to follow. He was angry and sent me abusive messages but he stayed away. A few weeks later I was shopping in town on my own and I saw him. He attacked me in the street in front of witnesses, and when someone rang the police he ran away. I was taken to hospital and a police officer came to visit me. I decided to make a statement and press charges. The police were great, very sensitive and considerate. Photos were taken of my injuries and my statement was recorded, in addition to the witness statements. He was arrested and as part of his bail conditions stated he could not contact me.

I thought this was the end of the ordeal, and although there was never any more violence the trauma and stress continued with court sessions being adjourned. Due to the overwhelming evidence against him he pleaded guilty. I was struggling with depression and decided to inform my line manager as we had developed a good relationship and I felt I could trust her. I also wanted my line manager to know because I didn't want her to suspect or think I couldn't cope with my teaching time table and classes, because that wasn't the problem.

After revealing my experience with domestic violence, my line manager was sympathetic for a brief moment then became judgmental and that familiar look of disbelief became apparent. I recall comments about how women can be so stupid to put up with abuse from men and stay in violent relationships for too long. I was devastated because I was hearing this from friends and family and regularly being hard on myself for staying in a toxic and abusive relationship.

My line manager informed the Headteacher and a meeting was scheduled. I felt sick with nerves and wondered if I would lose my job because I was a terrible judge of character. To my surprise, my Headteacher was amazing. She was very kind, understanding and not judgmental. She offered me support, told me about occupational health and other services that could assist if I needed it and told me her door was always open. This kindness was unexpected, overwhelming and something I will never forget.

My former partner was sentenced to probation with a restraining order to stay away from me and not contact me. The conviction for domestic violence was added *to his criminal record. He moved away and I have not seen him in over a decade. I have moved on but I continue to struggle with depression and anxiety.*

There are several reasons why I wish to remain anonymous for this case study. Firstly, I don't wish to be named to avoid any further conflict and hassle with my ex-partner. That chapter in my life is closed. I don't wish for him to know I have written about my experience to potentially provoke him and make him angry. I have to put my own safety and the safety of my family first.

Secondly, I am now a senior leader at a different school and I am proud of the success I have achieved. I do not want to be defined by domestic violence. I was a victim but I am now a survivor. I am happily married and have two children. Despite my anonymity I do appreciate the opportunity to write about domestic violence because people, including other women, can be very quick to judge and criticise instead of offering support and care.

There are many reasons women remain in abusive relationships. They can be too scared to leave out of fear of the consequences after threats are made. Another reason could be love and the belief or hope that people can change and forgiveness is possible. When there are children involved that can add other challenges as the partner will have parental rights to see the child/children. There could be financial reasons making it difficult for a woman to leave an abusive relationship. None of those reasons are excuses or justifications for remaining with an abusive partner, but it is complicated and every individual situation is unique.

If you experience domestic violence, my advice would be to find someone kind to talk and reach out to, because help is available. If you suspect a colleague could be the victim of domestic violence or you know this to be true, it is vital to be kind and supportive not judgmental or blunt. The first instinct might be to tell the woman to leave or question their reasons for staying but that is likely to add further pressure, stress and upset at an already difficult time.

Thank you to the contributor for sharing their experiences and advice.

Menopause

Menopause usually occurs for women between the ages of 45 and 55, but there are other factors that can induce early menopause (including surgery, hysterectomy or other sometimes unknown reasons). Menopause occurs when a woman has not experienced a period for twelve months. Perimenopause is the experience of menopausal symptoms before periods have stopped. This can be a very difficult combination of menopause symptoms whilst still experiencing the menstrual cycle.

It is important for all staff to be educated about the experience and impact of menopause. Increased awareness can lead to increased understanding, empathy and support.

On 18 October (World Menopause Day) 2021, Teacher Tapp asked its users the following question:

Q. How is your school supporting the menopause?

The findings from the survey revealed that only 5% of respondents said their school had a policy for supporting menopausal women, although many people did not know whether a policy focusing on menopause existed in their school. Teacher Tapp added:

> *The group who were most confident in their policies were headteachers. 15% of heads said that they do have a policy to support menopausal women. 15% is much greater than the 3% of classroom teachers who said their school did have a policy. The difference in percentages suggests that you may be in a school where a policy exists but you don't know about it!*

It is important that all staff are familiar with the policies and support in place.

Teacher Tapp asked the same question a year later in 2022 about a policy for supporting menopausal women in school, and the results had increased from 5% to 16% of users responding that their school did have a menopause policy. Increased awareness and discussion of menopause has come about as a result of organisations in education such as WomenEd and Teacher Tapp bringing it to the attention of school leaders. There have also been celebrity campaigners that have publicly spoken about menopause and are trying to break the taboo element of a natural human experience. An example of this is television host and personality Davina McCall. McCall hosted a Channel 4 documentary entitled *Davina McCall: Sex, myths and the menopause* and she has co-authored, with Dr Naomi Potter, the book, *Menopausing*.

Teacher Tapp also found, *'Requiring a policy to support menopausal women is popular among both genders of teachers'*. Two-thirds of voters agreed having a policy to support menopausal women should be required by schools. Teacher Tapp found the idea of a menopause policy was slightly more popular among female teachers than male.[14] Does your school have a menopause policy? Are you aware of this? This is not only relevant for women pre-menopause and during the menopause but also leaders at all levels should be informed, so as line managers they can support colleagues who experience menopause as best they can.

Bereavement

Bereavement can affect anyone. Across a school community it is highly likely there will be staff and students that have experienced the loss of a loved one. The death of a member of the school community, student or staff member, can have a very significant impact on the community.

This book is dedicated to my grandmother Hazel Pearson. I made the decision to dedicate the book to her prior to writing because I knew it is a special book that should be dedicated to a special woman in my life. When I began writing this book, despite some issues with mobility, my Gran Hazel was in considerably good health for her age at 87. In February 2023 my Gran experienced an unexpected brain aneurysm and died shortly after.

I am devastated by the loss of my Gran. Experiencing a bereavement during pregnancy has also been very difficult, with a range of emotions. Although the death of an elderly grandparent is to be expected and considered inevitable, it can still be very distressing and upsetting, as I have found.

I am an ambassador for Winston's Wish, a registered childhood bereavement charity in the UK. Their aim is to offer support and guidance to bereaved children and their families and schools. This is another essential area of training that is often neglected. It is highly likely teachers will have to support children that experience bereavement yet the necessary training and guidance is not always provided for teachers and leaders. To find out more about the services and the support Winston's Wish can offer, visit their website https://www.winstonswish.org/.

Experiencing the death of a loved one can be the biggest challenge an individual can face in their lifetime. This could be a close family member from a parent, sibling, grandparent, partner or child and the impact can be devastating. There is no set amount of time required to grieve as every individual and every experience is different. A bereavement policy in place at a school should be flexible to adapt to the needs of staff and students.

The circumstances of the death can also compound grief. This can vary from supporting a loved one through a terminal illness or the death can be an abrupt shock due to a tragic accident. Death by suicide is very different and can bring with it a range of complex emotions. Bereavement can be very emotionally and physically challenging.

Emotions can vary from sadness, anger, despair, frustration, guilt, anxiety and much more. Physical symptoms associated with bereavement can include anxiety, reduced or increased appetite, sleeplessness as well as feelings of fatigue and exhaustion. Consider how challenging work, and teaching in particular, would be whilst experiencing a combination of mental and physical health challenges.

For anyone struggling with grief there is support available. Talking to a colleague, line manager or senior leader honestly and openly may be difficult but it can help the school to help you. When trying to support someone in the workplace that has been bereaved, consider the following:

- **Acknowledge their loss.** It can be difficult to know what to say and it may feel like there are no right words, or the fear of saying the wrong thing. However, their loss should not be ignored but recognised in some way. This can be a brief comment offering support or communicated via a sympathy card or message to show they are in your thoughts.

- **Do not compare grief.** Every individual experiences grief differently. Comparisons are not helpful.

- **Be prepared to be patient, supportive and accommodating.** Grief can be present for a long time or it may come and go for others. There is no specific formula or protocol but kindness and empathy are key.

- **Avoid comments that undermine their loss.** Examples of this can include, '*at least they didn't have to suffer for long*' or '*at least they lived to a good age*'. Whilst these may be true and well intentioned often they are not helpful.

To find out more about how to support bereaved colleagues in the workplace, the registered charity Cruse Bereavement Support offer advice and guidance on their website https://www.cruse.org.uk/. There is also the option to complete training on bereavement through Cruse or Winston's Wish.

What can men do and what does it mean to be an ally?

A common misconception about feminism is the belief that women hate men or are against men. This is incorrect and should always be challenged. Feminism does not require men to be hated. It is essential men support women and are with us, not against us. They should be present when discussing issues such as the GPG, female representation in leadership, maternity and other issues specific to women.

Singer Beyoncé commented on the global GPG in The Shriver Report published in 2014, writing:

> We need to stop buying into the myth about gender equality. It isn't a reality yet. Today, women make up half of the U.S. workforce, but the average working woman earns only 77 percent of what the average working man makes. But unless women and men both say this is unacceptable, things will not change. Men have to demand that their wives, daughters, mothers, and sisters earn more—commensurate with their qualifications and not their gender. Equality will be achieved when men and women are granted equal pay and equal respect.[15]

Beyoncé is just one of many celebrities to be vocal about gender inequalities that exist and the role men must play if change is to happen.

Interview with Patrick Ottley-O'Connor

Bio: Following a teaching career spanning five decades, including nineteen successful years as a Principal/Executive Principal in secondary, primary and special schools, Patrick continues to share his expertise, experience and enthusiasm to support the education system as a leadership development coach for many aspiring, new/experienced headteachers, CEOs and other MAT leaders, particularly those facing significant challenge both in the UK and internationally.

Patrick leads and facilitates a variety of leadership programmes, including the National Professional Qualification for Headship (NPQH), National Professional Qualification for Executive Leadership (NPQEL) and other Executive Leadership programmes. He is a regular keynote speaker and skilled facilitator at educational leadership conferences and guest lectures on a range of Master's programmes. He actively uses his allyship and advocacy to champion diversity, equity and inclusion within education leadership, and to date has coached sixty plus women into headship. Patrick is married to Mel and has five sons. He is active on Twitter @ottleyoconnor.

Q1. Can you tell us why you think it is important for men involved in education to support and empower women in education?

Gender equality and the rights of women are not just an issue for women, they are an issue of human rights; consequently, it should be as big an issue for men as it is for women. It is the responsibility of all genders. It is important for men in education to strive for gender equality, as well as to support, encourage, engage and empower women in education. For much of my adult life I have actively promoted a culture of inclusion and equity in my schools through my intentional and conscious efforts to benefit individuals and groups of women. In short, I believe if men are not part of the solution, then they are part of the problem!

In September 2014 Emma Watson launched the HeForShe movement at the United Nations as a global solidarity movement for gender equality. It aligned with my ambition for boys and men to positively engage with and support gender equality. I signed the pledge and decided to take more positive action than merely being vocally supportive. Since then I have stepped up my active allyship through coaching, mentoring, sponsoring and supporting women. The creation of communities like WomenEd and Diverse Educators have provided me with a platform to work and grow as an ally alongside women in education.

Q2. What are the potential mistakes male staff members and school leaders can make when working alongside female colleagues?

Allyship intentions can be easily misguided and result in men being viewed and discounted as 'male saviours' and/or 'mansplainers'. The evolution of my allyship with women has been a lifelong process of building relationships based on trust, consistency and accountability with women. It has provided great opportunities for my personal growth and learning, whilst building confidence in others. My allyship is not self-defined. Intersectionality can greatly affect how my allyship manifests itself; consequently, I endeavour to ensure that my allyship is welcomed, recognised and embraced by the women that I ally with.

With hindsight, my allyship as a young teacher was that of a stereotypical male saviour and/or ally standing on the side-lines. I recall as a 28-year-old Assistant Headteacher becoming increasingly uncomfortable with the sexist behaviour of some male colleagues. I decided to publicly call out their sexist language in the staff room. It resulted in me losing 'friends', but I immediately felt liberated by being true to my beliefs and emerging and developing moral purpose. Since then and throughout my leadership journey, I have developed my own values-based vision for equality, inclusion and diversity, shaped by the strong women role models that have surrounded me.

Whenever I'm invited to speak at conferences and events or write publicly about my allyship as HeForShe, I discuss with women how best to support them with the community I seek to serve. This has been invaluable in providing advice on what they actually want from me as an ally and has often introduced me to different perspectives and a range of other resources and/or viewpoints.

Q3. How can male colleagues and school leaders learn more about supporting female colleagues?

It is important that school leaders build diverse, inclusive and equitable professional learning networks to build a healthy perspective and approach to allyship. I actively use Twitter as a platform to engage with a wide range of voices; in particular groups like @WomenEd, @DiverseEd2020, @LGBTedUK, @BAMEedNetwork and @DisabilityEdUK provide great opportunities for me to connect and learn more about supporting female colleagues.

Q4. How do you support women in your school community?

In my position of privilege as a male school leader, I was able to call out unacceptable behaviour towards women and importantly make my voice heard. In my schools, I regularly talked loudly and proudly about my HeForShe allyship and actively created a culture of care that embraced equality, inclusion and diversity that provided multiple opportunities for women's voices to be listened to and more importantly heard. Women in my schools told me that they were encouraged, engaged and empowered with equitable CPD/career opportunities and experiences. They also reported that they were more comfortable raising issues without a fear of backlash or risk of jeopardising professional relationships and/or career opportunities and development.

Now outside of direct school leadership, I make a continual investment of time in supporting others and championing women from the education community to support career growth. In the past few years I have voluntarily coached sixty plus women into headship and CEO roles. In addition, I actively encourage other men to join the growing HeForShe allyship movement. Words without actions are detrimental and work against changing the culture.

I have learned that there are several simple ways to support women as an ally in a school community. I strive to model my actions every day to be a HeForShe ally by:

- *Advocating and amplifying the voices, actions and achievements of women*

- *Ensuring equitable and accessible talent growth opportunities and experiences with women*

- *Welcoming and providing opportunities for women to vent and not viewing it as a personal attack on me*

- *Recognising, understanding and acknowledging the systematic inequalities faced by women in education and indeed general*

- *Using more inclusive language and being aware of gendered terms*

- *Believing the lived experiences of women*

- *Calling out inappropriate language and behaviour towards women*

- *Crucially, listening, supporting, self-reflecting and changing as I grow as an ally.*

Q5. You are an active #HeForShe ally. Why do you think it is necessary and important that more women are involved with senior school leadership?

It is a fact that the gender pay gap is real and that women are disproportionately underrepresented in school leadership positions. Despite the apparent shortage of school staff, I believe that there continues to be a great untapped reservoir of talented women seeking the right opportunities in schools with the right ethos. Women are constantly hindered by lack of accessible and equitable opportunity along with the host of barriers encountered, e.g. maternity, menopause, unconscious bias issues. To attract and retain women, leaders should review and adapt recruitment methods as well as talent development approaches and opportunities.

Finally, as an ally, my own learning, growth and addressing personal bias will not happen without being open to challenge. As an ally, I regularly listen to what women want from me, adapt my thinking, continually revisit and rework what I believe to be correct, and become more comfortable feeling uncomfortable in living my values as HeForShe.

Thank you to Patrick for his commitment and hard work towards empowering women in education and sharing his thoughts and advice in this book.

Women play a key role in their own journey, career progression and success. However, there are undeniable barriers that women continue to face. Together we can challenge, break and even smash these barriers with the hope for equity and equality for us and future generations of women.

The education sector is experiencing a number of challenges, impacting all those involved. Women dominate the teaching profession and experience additional challenges unique to women. Although women dominate the profession, they do not currently dominate leadership positions and the highest paid positions in education. Women do not dominate the education book sales and charts. Women are present at events and conferences but don't tend to dominate panels. Change is happening but there is much to be done to challenge and therefore promote further change.

This book is filled with case studies, interviews and spotlights on incredible and inspiring women in education. They are leading the way, and there are many other women that are fighting for change in our profession at a grassroots level. It is vital we all support each other because one woman alone cannot smash glass ceilings, it is something we do together.

#SmashingGlassCeilings

Help, guidance and further information

Bereavement support:

    https://www.cruse.org.uk/

    https://www.winstonswish.org/

    https://www.samaritans.org/

    https://www.nhs.uk/mental-health/feelings-symptoms-behaviours/feelings-and-symptoms/grief-bereavement-loss/

    https://www.thegoodgrieftrust.org/find-support/

    https://www.ataloss.org/

Miscarriage and still birth:

    https://www.miscarriageassociation.org.uk/

    https://www.tommys.org/

    https://www.sands.org.uk/

    https://petalscharity.org/miscarriage/

    https://www.miscarriageassociation.org.uk/

Domestic violence and abuse:

    https://www.womensaid.org.uk/

    https://www.gov.uk/guidance/domestic-abuse-how-to-get-help

    England: https://www.nationaldahelpline.org.uk/

    Wales: https://www.gov.wales/live-fear-free

    Scotland: https://www.sdafmh.org.uk/en/

    Northern Ireland: https://dsahelpline.org/

Sexual abuse:

    https://www.gov.uk/guidance/support-for-victims-of-sexual-violence-and-abuse

    https://sexualabusesupport.campaign.gov.uk/

    https://www.thesurvivorstrust.org/

    https://napac.org.uk/

Mental health, depression and anxiety:
https://www.educationsupport.org.uk/
https://www.mind.org.uk/
https://www.sane.org.uk/
https://togetherall.com/en-gb/
https://www.nhs.uk/mental-health/conditions/clinical-depression/support-groups/

LGBTQ+ support:
https://galop.org.uk/
https://lgbt.foundation/
https://mindout.org.uk/
https://switchboard.lgbt/
https://www.transunite.co.uk/
http://www.beaumontsociety.org.uk/

Endnotes

1 https://www.theguardian.com/world/2023/jan/19/jacinda-ardern-resigns-as-prime-minister-of-new-zealand

2 Hamilton, Dr David. (2019). *The little book of kindness: Connect with others, be happier, transform your life.* Page 7.

3 https://www.psychologytoday.com/intl/blog/the-gift-adhd/201108/being-nice-can-change-your-brain.

4 Alden, Lynn E., & Trew, Jennifer L. (2012). *If it makes you happy: Engaging in kind acts increases positive affect in socially anxious individuals.*

5 https://civilservice.blog.gov.uk/2022/05/19/why-weve-stopped-using-the-term-bame-in-government/

6 https://www.theguardian.com/education/2020/dec/14/almost-half-of-english-schools-have-no-bame-teachers-study-finds

7 https://www.gov.uk/working-when-pregnant-your-rights

8 https://www.nhs.uk/conditions/miscarriage/

9 Brearley, Joeli. (2021). *The motherhood penalty: How to stop motherhood being the kiss of death for your career.* Page 2.

10 Joeli Brearley. (2021) The Motherhood Penalty: How to stop motherhood being the kiss of death for your career. Page 3.

11 https://www.mtpt.org.uk/

12 https://www.bbc.co.uk/news/uk-england-surrey-64813551

13 https://www.bbc.co.uk/news/uk-64125045

14 https://teachertapp.co.uk/articles/what-does-your-school-do-to-support-the-menopause-this-health-and-safety-measures-and-parents-evenings/

15 https://shriverreport.org/gender-equality-is-a-myth-beyonce/

References

Introduction

https://www.womenscolleges.org/history

https://www.womenshistory.org/articles/why-are-so-many-teachers-women

https://explore-education-statistics.service.gov.uk/find-statistics/school-workforce-in-england

https://www.gov.scot/publications/summary-statistics-for-schools-in-scotland-2022/pages/school-teachers/

https://www.statista.com/statistics/718481/number-of-schools-in-scotland/

https://www.ewc.wales/site/index.php/en/research-and-statistics/workforce-statistics.html

https://www.education-ni.gov.uk/publications/teacher-workforce-statistics-202122

https://www.education-ni.gov.uk/sites/default/files/publications/education/Teacher%20workforce%20statistical%20infographic%20202122.PDF

https://www.gov.uk/government/news/uk-gender-pay-gap

Chapter 1

https://www.nfer.ac.uk/key-topics-expertise/school-workforce/teacher-recruitment-and-retention-in-england-data-dashboard

Chapter 2

https://schoolsweek.co.uk/the-emerging-super-league-of-academy-trust-ceo-pay/

https://schoolsweek.co.uk/best-paid-trust-ceos-wages-rise-fastest-but-some-rein-in-pay/

https://corporatetrainingmaterials.com/blogs/using-our-materials/internationals-womens-day.

https://schoolsweek.co.uk/revealed-the-lack-of-diversity-in-education-leadership-roles/

https://www.gov.uk/guidance/women-leading-in-education-regional-networks

https://womened.org/about-us

Coe, R., Kime, S., & Singleton, D. (2022). *School environment and leadership: Evidence review.*

Chapter 3

Coe, R., Rauch, C.J., Kime, S., & Singleton, D. (2020). *The great teaching toolkit: Evidence review*. https://evidencebased.education/greatteaching-toolkit/

https://educationendowmentfoundation.org.uk/news/eef-publishes-new-guidance-on-professional-development

Chapter 4

https://www.mckinsey.com/featured-insights/mckinsey-explainers/what-is-innovation

https://www.forbes.com/sites/forbesbusinesscouncil/2019/12/30/back-to-basics-what-is-innovation/

https://teachertapp.co.uk/

https://www.bbc.co.uk/news/business-46470428

Chapter 6

https://twitter.com/dylanwiliam/status/1571954811234586624

Chapter 7

https://www.avocadosocial.com/uk-social-media-statistics-2022/

https://www.bbc.co.uk/news/education-59264238

https://www.nasuwt.org.uk/advice/health-safety/social-media-and-online-abuse-of-teachers.html

https://teachertapp.co.uk/articles/curriculum-intent-social-media-regulation-and-the-teacher-tapp-upgrade/

https://rightsofwomen.org.uk/news/rights-of-women-survey-reveals-online-sexual-harassment-has-increased-as-women-continue-to-suffer-sexual-harassment-whilst-working-through-the-covid-19-pandemic/

https://www.gov.uk/government/news/cyberflashing-to-become-a-criminal-offence

https://www.transactual.org.uk/trans-lives-21

Chapter 8

https://www.theguardian.com/world/2023/jan/19/jacinda-ardern-resigns-as-prime-minister-of-new-zealand

Hamilton, Dr David. (2019). *The little book of kindness: Connect with others, be happier, transform your life*. Page 7.

https://www.psychologytoday.com/intl/blog/the-gift-adhd/201108/being-nice-can-change-your-brain

Alden, Lynn E., & Trew, Jennifer L. (2012). *If it makes you happy: Engaging in kind acts increases positive affect in socially anxious individuals.*

https://civilservice.blog.gov.uk/2022/05/19/why-weve-stopped-using-the-term-bame-in-government/

https://www.theguardian.com/education/2020/dec/14/almost-half-of-english-schools-have-no-bame-teachers-study-finds

https://www.gov.uk/working-when-pregnant-your-rights

https://www.nhs.uk/conditions/miscarriage/

Brearley, Joeli. (2021). *The motherhood penalty: How to stop motherhood being the kiss of death for your career.*

https://www.mtpt.org.uk/

https://www.bbc.co.uk/news/uk-england-surrey-64813551

https://www.bbc.co.uk/news/uk-64125045

https://teachertapp.co.uk/articles/what-does-your-school-do-to-support-the-menopause-this-health-and-safety-measures-and-parents-evenings/

https://www.winstonswish.org/

https://www.cruse.org.uk/

https://shriverreport.org/gender-equality-is-a-myth-beyonce/

Index

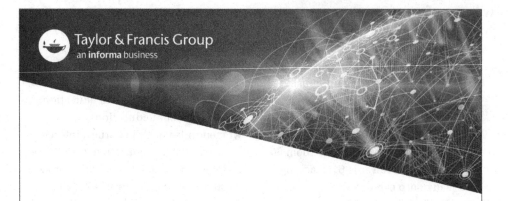

Printed in the United States
by Baker & Taylor Publisher Services